Teacher's Guide

Yellow Level

Copyright © 2013 by HMH Supplemental Publishers Inc.

All rights reserved. No part of this work may be reproduced or transmitted in any form or by any means, electronic or mechanical, including photocopying or recording, or by any information storage or retrieval system, without the prior written permission of the copyright owner unless such copying is expressly permitted by federal copyright law.

Permission is hereby granted to teachers to photocopy entire pages from this publication in classroom quantities for instructional use and not for resale. Requests for information on other matters regarding duplication of this work should be addressed to Houghton Mifflin Harcourt Publishing Company, Attn: Contracts, Copyrights, and Licensing, 9400 Southpark Center Loop, Orlando, Florida 32819-8647.

Common Core State Standards © Copyright 2010. National Governors Association Center for Best Practices and Council of Chief State School Officers. All rights reserved.
This product is not sponsored or endorsed by the Common Core State Standards Initiative of the National Governors Association Center for Best Practices and the Council of Chief State School Officers.

Printed in the U.S.A.

ISBN 978-0-547-99055-2

1 2 3 4 5 6 7 8 9 10   2266   21 20 19 18 17 16 15 14 13 12

4500377511   A B C D E F G

If you have received these materials as examination copies free of charge, Houghton Mifflin Harcourt Publishing Company retains title to the materials and they may not be resold. Resale of examination copies is strictly prohibited.

Possession of this publication in print format does not entitle users to convert this publication, or any portion of it, into electronic format.

Contents

PM Stars Extensions iv
Core Components vi
Instructional Path viii
PM Stars Fiction x
PM Stars Nonfiction xii
PM Stars Teacher's Guide xiv
Yellow Level Scope and Sequence xviii

Lessons

Monkey's Skateboard 2

Josh's Shop 8

Sit Down, Socks! 14

Jet Is Naughty 20

Pokey Is Sick 26

Jolly Roger and the Coconuts 32

The Town Garden 38

The Big Ship 44

Telephones 50

Small Animals that Hide 56

Our Vegetable Garden 62

Meg's Family 68

Making a Toy Telephone 74

Making a Little Raft 80

Looking for Frogs 86

Kris's Family 92

Cam's Family 98

Anna's Family 104

Extensions

Supportive texts and best-practice instruction combined in a stellar series that features...

☆ favorite and new recurring characters across fiction and nonfiction

☆ meticulous text leveling with a controlled introduction of new words

☆ support for foundational reading skills and acquisition of reading vocabulary

☆ a focus on strategies for building text comprehension

☆ informal assessment and progress monitoring

Core Components

Step-by-step lessons offer supportive, rigorous instruction in comprehension, phonics, fluency, and writing.

The PM Stars Teacher's Guide includes:

- Guided reading prompts to aid comprehension of leveled reading texts.
- Supportive instruction for guiding children in skill development.
- Graphic organizers to support vocabulary and comprehension skill acquisition.

Companion Resources

Additional PM resources build a powerful solution for differentiating and documenting learning.

PM Ultra Benchmark Kit is an effective assessment tool for Grades K–5 used to place children in the appropriate level of the PM Family series. Assessment data can be entered into the Rigby PM Data Management Tool for classroom, school, and district use.

The PM Stars Yellow Level includes:

- 18 student titles
- PM Levels 6 through 9
- 12 nonfiction texts
- 6 fiction texts

My PM Word Book is a consumable product featuring PM vocabulary words—and places for children to record their own words—to be used as support for reading and writing.

PM High-Frequency Word Cards include everything needed to help children learn critical high-frequency words at school and home—building a foundation for reading success!

Yellow Level vii

Instructional Path

PM Stars builds foundational reading skills and comprehension with a consistent, easy-to-use instructional routine.

① Before Reading

- Guide children in previewing the book, focusing on accessing background information.

- Support foundational reading by building important phonics and fluency skills.

- Introduce critical comprehension skills, such as making inferences and identifying author's purpose.

② Reading the Text

- Lead children in a guided reading session, focusing on critical comprehension and application of key skills.

- Support early and emergent readers as they learn and apply important reading strategies, such as looking for known words and checking for patterns.

- Utilize point-of-use instruction and questions to make reading strategies relevant as children read.

- Guide children to read independently as you observe, making note of children's mastery of skills taught in the lesson.

③ Review

- Review the key skills taught in the lesson, paying close attention to children's application of vocabulary, phonics, fluency, and comprehension skills.

- Guide children in developing a writing product connected to their reading. Support children in using a key writing skill, such as naming a topic and developing a conclusion.

④ Assessment

- Guide children in quick, informal assessment activities to showcase their understanding of the key skills practiced in the lesson.

Yellow Level ix

PM Stars Fiction

Favorite recurring characters, along with some new friends, draw readers into the text.

☆ PM Stars fiction books feature engaging narratives with clear plots and interesting characters.

☆ Recurring characters provide a foundation of background knowledge and keep children engaged in the reading.

☆ Strong text-to-picture matches guide children in comprehending as they read.

☆ Careful leveling, including a steady growth in sentence complexity, supports readers in making incremental progress.

Click! Click! Click!

Look, Harry.

Here comes the little robot.

☆ A systematic inclusion of high-frequency words supports young readers in developing their word knowledge.

PM Stars Nonfiction

Nonfiction books build skills across a variety of genres, including informational reports, procedural texts, and personal narratives.

☆ Text features, such as labels, headings, and glossaries, expose readers to critical aspects of reading nonfiction texts.

☆ The gradual introduction of new vocabulary words—a ratio of 1 to 20, in both fiction and nonfiction—guide students in building their personal word stores.

The Race

Milly and Kate went in my race.

We went up to the **line**.

The teacher said, "Go!"

6

☆ Interesting nonfiction topics, such as science, social studies, and the arts, capture readers' interest.

☆ 8 nonfiction books explore recurring themes:
- Travel and Transport
- Protection and Covering
- Communication and Technology
- Leisure and Work

☆ 4 nonfiction books follow a cast of recurring family characters, including:
- Cam's family
- Meg's family
- Kris's family
- Anna's family

PM Stars Teacher's Guide
Clear, predictable support for foundational reading skills and comprehension . . .

A lesson overview provides a listing of lesson targets and learning objectives.

Additional titles within the same theme or featuring the same characters provide opportunities for text-to-text connections.

Vocabulary activities help set a foundation for comprehending key ideas in the book.

Reading Word Count: 170

Small Animals that Hide
Written by Elsie Nelley

Overview Many small animals have to hide to protect themselves. What are they hiding from? Where do they hide?
Reading Vocabulary Words hide p. 2, safe p. 3, fox p. 6, coat p. 6, insect p. 8, shell p. 10, pouch p. 14
Phonics Skill Consonant digraph *th*
Fluency Point Voice falling at end of declarative sentence
Comprehension Strategy Using text features
Reading Strategy Pointing to each word as you read
Writing Connection Book review
Common Core State Standards RI.1.5 Know and use various text features to locate key facts or information in a text; RF.1.3a Know the spelling-sound correspondences for common consonant digraphs; RF.1.4 Read grade-level text orally with accuracy, appropriate rate, and expression; W.1.1 Write opinion pieces in which they introduce the topic or name the book they are writing about, state an opinion, supply a reason for the opinion, and provide some sense of closure; L.1.5c Identify real-life connections between words and their use.

High-Frequency Words

stay   white
of   like

More books within the protection and covering theme
Our Sunhats
PM Stars Red Levels 5/6
Making a Sunhat
PM Stars Red Levels 5/6
Looking for Frogs
PM Stars Red Levels 8/9
Big Animals That Hide
PM Stars Blue Levels 11/12
A Firefighter
PM Stars Green Levels 14/15

1 Before Reading

Build Background
- Read aloud the title with children. Point out the author's name. Say *This book is about small animals hiding.* Invite children to predict why small animals need to hide.
- Have children tell what they know about small animals. Explain that animals might hide from people or from other animals that want to eat them. Say *Where might a small animal hide?*

Focus on Reading Vocabulary
- Write each vocabulary word on chart paper, reading it aloud as you write it. Have children read the words with you. Ask children these questions: *Which word names an animal that has fur? Which word means that you are away from harm? Which word names an animal with six legs? Which word names something you can do? Which word names clothing? Which word names a type of covering? Which word names a place where a baby kangaroo can hide?*
- Explain to children that by making connections between words and ideas, we build vocabulary skills. Connections between vocabulary words make the process of building vocabulary skills faster and more efficient. Say *Sometimes a word reminds me of other things or makes me think of something else.* Write the word *coat* on chart paper. Have children repeat the word. Ask *What does the word coat remind you of?*

☆ Instruction in phonics and fluency supports foundational reading skills that apply to the book.

☆ Activities target potential roadblocks for ESL/ELL students.

- Model filling in a Connections chart. Write *coat* in the circle. Brainstorm with children what this word reminds them of, what it makes them think of, things they've heard about, and things they've seen.

Focus on Phonics
Write the word *that* on chart paper. Explain that sometimes two consonants make a single sound. Say *When t and h are together, they make the sound /th/*. Point out the *t* and *h* and say */th/*. Then say *that*. Write the words *the* and *they* on chart paper. Have children read each word and identify the digraph *th* in each.

Focus on Fluency
On the board, write a declarative sentence, such as *Every tiger has a different pattern in its fur.* Say *The period at the end of this sentence means I am telling you something. When you see a period at the end of a sentence, your voice should drop, or become lower.* Read the sentence aloud for children. Have the children repeat the sentence after you.

Focus on Comprehension
Explain that some nonfiction books include special features called a Contents page and headings. Tell children that using text features helps them understand information in the book. Direct children to look at the Contents page of *Small Animals that Hide*. Explain that a Contents page lists the sections of a book and the page number where each begins. Ask a volunteer to tell the page where one section begins. Turn to that section and point to the heading. Say *This is a heading. The heading tells what you will learn in that section of the book.*

2 Reading the Text

Have children read the book. As appropriate, monitor application of the comprehension strategy and support strategic reading using the prompts below.

Pages 2–3   Say *Name two details that you read about small animals.* Ask *What makes the hiding animals difficult to see?*

Pages 4–5   Say *Look at the top of page 4.* Ask *What is the heading of this section of the book? Where else do you see this heading? How is the Contents page helpful?* Guide children to understand that the Contents page makes it easy to find information in a text.

Pages 6–7   Ask *What is the heading for this section of the book? What do you think the author wants us to understand about color?* Have children point to a period and explain how to read the sentence.

Pages 8–9   Say *What did you learn about the shape of this small animal?* Point to the word *insect*. Say *How is an insect different from a fox? How are they the same?*

ESL/ELL
Different languages have different sounds. Some children may not be familiar with the /th/ sound. Demonstrate making the sound for children as you push your tongue between your teeth. Invite them to repeat after you. Have children take turns pronouncing such words as *thank, thin, thick,* and *thump*.

Reading Strategy
Explain to children that sometimes when they have difficulty reading, they should reread and point to each word to help make sense of the text. This will also help make sure that they don't miss any words. Say *When you point to each word as you read, you make sure you don't miss anything.*

☆ Explicit instruction in a comprehension concept provides a strategic focus for reading the text.

☆ Prompts, questions, and tips support key lesson concepts.

Yellow **Levels 8/9** 57

Yellow Level **xv**

PM Stars Teacher's Guide

☆ Independent practice encourages application of the target comprehension skill and provides an opportunity for informal assessment.

☆ Structured review activities reinforce lesson objectives.

High-Frequency Words
For children who need additional practice, use the appropriate cards from the *PM High-Frequency Word Cards* boxed set. Pair children and have them practice writing the high-frequency words.

Visual Literacy
Ask students to choose three to five images that, together, best summarize the text. Then pair students and have them take turns explaining their choices.

Pages 10–11 Point out that *shell* is boldfaced and that it is an important word for this topic. Have children find out more about the word in the glossary.

Pages 12–13 Ask *What is the heading for this section of* Small Animals that Hide? *How does the shape of a crab help it hide?*

Pages 14–15 Ask *Do you see a word that has letters th? Say the word* mother *and listen for the sound made by letters* th.. Point out the boldfaced word *pouch.* Ask *Why do you think this word is in bold type? Show me the text feature where I can find out more about the word.*

● **Independent Practice**
To further support application of the comprehension skill, have children reread the book using the Text Feature graphic organizer for support. Work with children to write *Contents* or *Heading* in the top box and to write how the text feature helps them in the bottom box. Observe children as they read. Make note, mentally or in writing, how each child is or is not using the skills and strategies being focused on in this lesson.

●  **3 Review**

Reading Vocabulary
- Remind children that when they make connections between words and ideas, they are building vocabulary skills. Say *The more you think about words and how they are connected, the more you will understand about their meanings.* Write *safe, hide,* and *pouch* on the board. Have children choose one word and complete a Connections graphic organizer.
- Have children highlight or add the reading vocabulary words in their copies of *My PM Word Book.* Encourage children to use these words in their writing.

Phonics
Have children find and list words from *Small Animals that Hide* that begin with *th* in the text. (*that, the, they*)

Fluency
With a partner, have children take turns rereading pages 14 and 15, focusing on dropping their voices when they see a period at the end of a sentence.

Comprehension
Ask children to refer to their completed Text Feature graphic organizers for *Small Animals that Hide* as you lead a discussion about text features. Review specific information about a contents page, headings, boldfaced words, and a glossary.

☆ A writing connection extends text comprehension and also supports key writing concepts.

☆ Differentiated instruction provides options for students with different learning styles.

Writing Connection
- Tell children they will write a book review about *Small Animals that Hide*. Explain that a book review is not a retelling of the book. A book review gives readers an idea of what a book is like and whether or not the reviewer enjoyed it. Provide the following guide to assist children in their writing:
  I read _____ .
  It is about _____ .
  The book is _____ because _____ .
  I think you will _____ .
- Explain that the book review will name the book, which is the topic of the review. It will include an opinion about the book and give a reason for the opinion. Discuss with children why they liked or disliked about *Small Animals that Hide* using specific examples. Remind children that the last part of their review leaves the reader with a feeling of "completeness."

4 Assessment

Phonics
Write *sing, bank, pick,* and *win* on the board. Have children write each word replacing the beginning letter with digraph *th* and read the new word.

Fluency
Individually, have children read pages 10 and 14 aloud. Check to make sure that each child drops his or her voice when they come to a period at the end of a sentence.

Comprehension
Review each child's Text Feature graphic organizer, prompting children to explain the comprehension strategy and to talk through the graphic organizer.

Differentiated Instruction
- **Tactile** learners can "feel" the words by placing a pretend green frog on a piece of green paper.
- **Auditory** learners can "hear" the words by working with partners and listening as one partner reads the text.
- **Visual** learners can "see" the words by looking at pictures of other small animals.

☆ Assessment activities gauge student learning and inform future instruction.

PM Stars Yellow Level • Scope and Sequence

Title	Fiction/Nonfiction	Running Words	Comprehension Skill
Monkey's Skateboard	Fiction	119	Explaining differences between books
Josh's Shop	Fiction	124	Asking and answering questions
Sit Down, Socks!	Fiction	138	Using illustrations and details to describe
Jet Is Naughty	Fiction	134	Using illustrations and details to describe
Pokey Is Sick	Fiction	150	Retelling story events or key details
Jolly Roger and the Coconuts	Fiction	150	Comparing and contrasting information
The Town Garden	Nonfiction	144	Identifying topic and key details
The Big Ship	Nonfiction	162	Describing connections within a text
Telephones	Nonfiction	149	Using text features

Phonics Skill	Fluency Skill	Writing Connection
Long vowel o	Changing voice to differentiate speakers	Book report
Multiple-syllable words	Voice rising at end of question	Story
Long vowel e	Matching character's tone	Narrative
Spelling pattern CVVC	Using loudness and softness to express emotion	Story
Multiple-syllable words	Matching character's voice	Story
Consonant digraph sh	Matching character's feelings and emotions	Book review
Spelling pattern CV	Reading smoothly	Explanation
Irregularly spelled words	Reading smoothly	Book review
Long vowels	Reading phrases as mini-sentences	Report

PM Stars Yellow Level • Scope and Sequence

Title	Fiction/Nonfiction	Running Words	Comprehension Skill
Small Animals that Hide	Nonfiction	167	Using text features
Our Vegetable Garden	Nonfiction	116	Identifying topic and key details
Meg's Family	Nonfiction	147	Identifying topic and key details
Making a Toy Telephone	Nonfiction	85	Distinguishing information from pictures and text
Making a Little Raft	Nonfiction	108	Distinguishing information from pictures and text
Looking for Frogs	Nonfiction	136	Using text features
Kris's Family	Nonfiction	158	Using text features
Cam's Family	Nonfiction	158	Asking and answering questions
Anna's Family	Nonfiction	164	Identifying main topic and key details

Phonemic Awareness/ Phonics Skill	Fluency Skill	Writing Connection
Consonant digraph *th*	Voice falling at end of declarative sentence	Book review
Consonant digraph *ch*	Reading smoothly	Explanation
Spelling pattern CVC*e*	Pausing at commas	Book review
Irregularly spelled words	Accurately pronouncing difficult words	Recommendation
Spelling pattern CVC	Reading phrases as mini-sentences	Recommendation
Inflected ending *-ed*	Voice falling at end of declarative sentence	Explanation
Inflected ending *-s*	Adjusting pace	Recommendation
Inflected ending *-ing*	Taking a breath at appropriate times	Personal narrative
Segmenting	Identifying main topic and key details	Report

Yellow Level xxi

Lessons

Monkey's Skateboard
Written by Annette Smith   Illustrated by Chantal Stewart

Overview Monkey has a skateboard. He lets Rabbit ride it. Little Teddy doesn't want to ride it because it's too big. He rides his bike instead. What do you think Monkey and Little Teddy will do together?

Reading Vocabulary Words monkey p. 2, skateboard p. 2, rabbit p. 6, bike p. 8, path p. 12

Phonics Skill Long vowel *o*

Fluency Point Changing voice to differentiate speakers

Comprehension Strategy Explaining differences between books

Reading Strategy Using your strategies

Writing Connection Book report

Common Core State Standards RL.1.5 Explain major differences between books that tell stories and books that give information, drawing on a wide reading of a range of text types; RF.1.3c Know finals -e and common vowel team conventions for representing long vowel sounds; RF.1.4b Read on-level text orally with accuracy, appropriate rate, and expression on successive readings; W.1.2 Write informative/explanatory texts in which they name a topic, supply some facts about the topic, and provide some sense of closure.

Reading Word Count: 119

High-Frequency Words

his	your
will	ride

More books within the character series

Little Teddy and Monkey
PM Stars Red Level 3

A Home for Little Teddy
PM Stars Red Level 5

The Boat Ride
PM Stars Magenta Level 2

1 Before Reading

Build Background

- Read aloud the title with children. Point out the author's and illustrator's names, talk about the cover illustration, and share the overview. Say *Monkey is on a skateboard. Does he look like he's having fun? Can real monkeys ride skateboards?* Invite children to point out details and make predictions.
- Have children tell what they know about skateboards. Ask *Have you ever tried to ride a skateboard? Was it hard to do? Why is the monkey on the skateboard wearing a helmet?*

Focus on Reading Vocabulary

- Write the vocabulary words on the board and have children read them aloud with you. Provide definitions. Ask children to make up sentences that include the words *monkey* and *rabbit*. Then have them make up sentences that include the words *skateboard, bike*, and *path*.
- Model filling in the Sentence Maker graphic organizer. In the top box, write this sentence starter *At the park, I saw a ____*. Use a vocabulary word to complete the sentence in the next box: *path*.

Focus on Phonics

Say *One vowel sound we know is the long o sound. Let's name words that have the long o sound.* Have children volunteer words. Write *so, boat,* and *cone* on chart paper. Read each word aloud, pointing out the different spelling patterns. Say *Each word has a different spelling pattern that makes the long vowel sound.*

Focus on Fluency

Say *Sometimes the characters in a story say things to other characters.* Point out that reading each character's words in a different voice helps listeners know which character speaks. Display a dialogue from a familiar fiction book. Read it aloud, changing your voice to differentiate speakers. Then have children echo your reading.

Focus on Comprehension

Say *Some books are written to entertain readers. These books are often about make-believe characters and the things they do. Other books are written to teach readers about something. They often have photographs of real things.* Display a fiction and a nonfiction book with a common topic, such as a book about real cats and one about a make-believe cat. Have children tell what elements the two books have in common and how they differ.

ESL/ELL

Give children paper cutouts of Monkey, Little Bear, and Rabbit. Help children use them to retell the story with you. You might act out the parts of Monkey and Rabbit and have children act out the part of Little Teddy.

2 Reading the Text

Have children read *Monkey's Skateboard*. As appropriate, monitor application of the comprehension strategy and support strategic reading using the prompts below.

Title page Say *This book does not list the contents. Do you think the book will tell information about a real skateboard? What would a book about a real skateboard be like?*

Pages 2–3 Say *How is the image on page 3 like images from other fiction books? How is it different from images in nonfiction books?* Ask *What do you think Monkey's voice sounds like? Use your voice to sound like Monkey as you read what he says.*

Pages 4–5 Have children locate what Little Teddy says. Ask *Should Little Teddy's voice sound the same as Monkey's voice?* Invite children to read Little Teddy's words in a voice different from Monkey's. Ask *What does Little Teddy tell about himself? What information would a book about a real bear cub tell?*

Pages 6–7 Ask *What does Rabbit do? How do real rabbits behave? How can you tell that this is a fiction book?*

Pages 8–9 Say *How would you describe the character of Little Teddy? How would you describe Monkey? How would you describe a real monkey?*

Reading Strategy

Explain to children that reading is more than just pronouncing words—it requires understanding. Tell them that readers use a variety of strategies to get meaning from text, such as looking at the pictures, looking at the first letter of the word, and using punctuation as you read. Have children discuss reading strategies they used as they read pages 6 and 7.

High-Frequency Words

For children who need additional practice, use the appropriate cards from the *PM High-Frequency Word Cards* boxed set. Have children use each word in a short sentence and practice reading the words and sentences aloud.

Visual Literacy

Have children look at the picture on page 11. How do these animals look and act like real people?

Pages 10–11 Ask *What do you think will happen next? Why?* Draw children's attention to the illustration. Ask *If this book were nonfiction, how would the image be different?*

Pages 12–13 Ask *What feature might a book about real animals have to give the meaning of* path? *Should this book have that feature? Why do you think so? Why not?*

Pages 14–15 Point out the word *Go*. Ask *What is the vowel sound in this word? Think about how the animals in this story move. How do real monkeys, rabbits, and bears move?*

Page 16 Have children identify the problem and solution in the story. Tell children that the story line is an element of fiction. Ask *What would the ending of a nonfiction book about animals be like?*

Independent Practice

To further support application of the comprehension skill, have children reread the book using the Fiction or Nonfiction graphic organizer for support. Have children describe one of the characters in this fiction story and what its real counterpart in a nonfiction book would be like. Observe children as they read. Make note of how each child is or is not using the skills and strategies being focused on in this lesson.

3 Review

Reading Vocabulary

- Select a word, such as *skateboard*, from this lesson's vocabulary skill and model filling in the Sentence Maker graphic organizer. Ask children to contribute ideas for the sentences.
- Have children highlight, or add, the reading vocabulary words in their copies of *My PM Word Book*. Encourage them to use the words in their writing.

Phonics

Write the following words on index cards: *mop, go, bone, hope, so, rock, no*. Ask children to read each word and identify its vowel sound. Have children sort the words into groups with common spelling patterns and discuss the patterns.

Fluency

Remind children to change their voices to sound like different characters. Have groups of three children practice by reading the parts of Monkey, Little Teddy, and Rabbit on pages 6 and 8.

Comprehension

Ask children to refer to their Fiction or Nonfiction graphic organizers for *Monkey's Skateboard* as you lead a discussion about the elements and features of fiction and nonfiction books.

Writing Connection

- Say *We write book reports to give information about a book, such as its title, author, and what the book is about.* Ask children to write a book report about *Monkey's Skateboard*. Guide them in noting the author and title of the story.
- Have children recall and retell what the book is about. Provide the following sentence frames to guide their writing:

    In the book, Monkey _____ .
    Then Rabbit _____ .
    Monkey wants Little Teddy to _____ .
    Finally they all _____ .

- Point out the last sentence frame as the closing, or ending. Remind children that the last part of their report is important. Encourage children to provide a sense of closure to their writing by including information about the end of the story, such as what the characters do at the end of the story.

4 Assessment

Phonics
Write this sentence on chart paper: *I have no socks.* Individually, have children read the sentence and then identify the word with long *o*.

Fluency
Individually, have children read page 4 aloud. Check to make sure that each child is changing his or her voice to differentiate characters.

Comprehension
Review each child's Fiction or Nonfiction graphic organizer, prompting the child to explain the comprehension strategy and to talk through the graphic organizer.

Differentiated Instruction

- **Kinesthetic** learners can "feel" the story by using puppets to act out the events of the story.
- **Auditory** learners can "hear" the story by listening to someone read the narrative while they read, differentiating the voices of Monkey, Little Teddy, and Rabbit.
- **Tactile** learners can "feel" the story by acting it out on a felt storyboard.

Character Spotlight

Monkey
Explain to children that all characters have special traits that make them what they are. Provide children with a brainstorming map with *Monkey* written in the center circle. Have them think about Monkey. As a group, brainstorm words that describe Monkey's traits and add these to the map.

Name_____

Sentence Maker

1.

2.

3.

Monkey's Skateboard PM Stars Teacher's Guide—Yellow Level

Name_____

Fiction or Nonfiction

Things I notice about nonfiction book

Things I notice about fiction book

Josh's Shop

Written by Annette Smith   Illustrated by Samantha Asri

Overview Lily wants to get food from Josh's shop. Josh doesn't have what Lily wants, but he does have a treat Lily likes. What does Josh's shop have?

Reading Vocabulary Words shop p. 2, bread p. 4, eggs p. 6, baby p. 8, bananas p. 8, hungry p. 12, ice cream p. 12

Vocabulary Skill Word sorts

Phonics Skill Multiple-syllable words

Fluency Point Voice rising at end of question

Comprehension Strategy Asking and answering questions

Reading Strategy Looking for words you know

Writing Connection Story

Common Core State Standards RL.1.1 Ask and answer questions about key details in a text; RF.1.3d Use knowledge that every syllable must have a vowel sound to determine the number of syllables in a printed word; RF.1.3e Decode two-syllable words following basic patterns by breaking the words into syllables; RF.1.4b Read grade-level text orally with accuracy, appropriate rate, and expression; W.1.3 Write narratives in which they recount two or more appropriately sequenced events, include some details regarding what happened, use temporal words to signal event order, and provide some sense of closure; L.1.5a Sort words into categories to gain a sense of the concepts the categories represent; L.1.5b Define words by category and by one or more key attributes.

Reading Word Count: 124

High-Frequency Words

good	this
I'm	your
today	will

More books within the character series

Lily's Apple
PM Stars Red Level 4

The Snow Bus
PM Stars Blue Level 10

1 Before Reading

Build Background

- Introduce the book by reading aloud the title with children. Point out the author's and illustrator's names. Say *Josh and Lily are playing pretend. What might Lily want to get at Josh's shop? Why might she want these things?* Invite children to point out details to support their responses.
- Have children tell what they know about shops. Ask *Why do people go to a shop? What would you buy in a toy shop? Where would you buy milk?*

Focus on Reading Vocabulary

- Write each Reading Vocabulary word on the board and read it aloud. Discuss with children what they know about each word, filling in any gaps in their understanding. Then have children use each word in a sentence.
- Explain that a category is a group of things that are alike in some way. Say *We can sort words into categories by thinking about how they are alike. Doing this helps us understand the words.* Have children generate categories that vocabulary words could fit into, like food, groceries, eating, etc. Then have them tell a key fact about each word, such as *A banana is a yellow fruit.*

- Model filling in a Word Sorter graphic organizer. Write the categories *Food* and *Not Food* in the two second-tier boxes. Working together, sort the vocabulary words into the boxes below the two categories.

Focus on Phonics

Explain to children that all syllables must have a vowel sound. Counting the vowel sounds in a printed word can help find the number of syllables. Write *lady* on chart paper. Say *La- is the first syllable and -dy is the second syllable.* Have children clap the word *lady* and count the two syllables. Work together to circle the vowel in each syllable. Point out that the number of vowel sounds and the number of syllables in the word are the same. Say *I see the consonant-vowel pattern in the last syllable. This pattern is said with a long vowel sound.* Practice saying the word. Then repeat with *pony* and *candy*. Guide children to notice consonant-vowel and consonant-vowel-consonant spelling patterns.

Focus on Fluency

Write *Can you see this?* on the board. Circle the question mark and have children identify it. Explain that the question mark shows that the sentence asks a question. Say *When you read a question, your voice rises, or goes up, at the end.* Read the question again and then have children read it chorally with you.

Focus on Comprehension

Explain to children that to better understand a story, they can ask questions about it and look for the answers as they read. Remind children about the question words *who, what, when, where, why,* and *how*. For example, they might ask themselves, *What does Josh sell in his shop?* Say *If you think of a question, look at the text and pictures to try to answer it. Asking and answering questions will help you understand what you read.*

2 Reading the Text

Have children read *Josh's Shop*. As appropriate, monitor application of the comprehension strategy and support strategic reading using the prompts below.

Pages 2–3 Say *Josh is pretending to be the shop owner. We can ask, who is Lily pretending to be?* Guide children to answer the question and tell how they know.

Pages 4–5 Ask *What is the first thing Lily asks for? Does Josh's shop have it?* Guide children to ask a question about what else Lily might be looking for. Say *We can keep reading to try to find the answer.*

Pages 6–7 Remind children of the last question asked on pages 4–5. Ask *Does this information answer the question?* Call on a volunteer to ask another question about the story. Tell children to look in the text and picture for the answer as they read on.

ESL/ELL

Write a question, such as *Where are you going?*, on the board. Read the question and point out the question mark. Ask children to share how questions are indicated in their home language. Provide support for them to ask a question orally and then help them write it, correctly placing a question mark at the end.

Reading Strategy

Explain to children that they can look for known words to help them when reading. Say *When you come to a word you don't know, use the words you do know to help figure it out.* Point out *ice cream* on page 14. Say *I don't know how to read these words, so I will look for other words I know.* Read the sentences aloud skipping over *ice cream*. Say *The words tell me that Josh gives something to Lily. When I look at the picture, I see Lily holding an ice cream.* Ice Cream *looks right and makes sense. The words I know helped me understand.*

Yellow **Level 6** 9

High-Frequency Words

For children who need additional practice, use the appropriate cards from the *PM High-Frequency Word Cards* boxed set. Pair children and have them take turns using the high-frequency words in oral sentences.

Visual Literacy

Have children look at the picture of Lily on page 9. Ask *Does Lily look happy or unhappy? How can you tell?* Have children redraw the character of Lily, changing the facial expression to represent a different emotion.

Pages 8–9 Ask *What does Lily's baby like to eat? Will she be able to eat bananas? Why?* Point to the question mark and ask *How do we read a question?* Have children read line 3 with proper inflection.

Pages 10–11 Read the page with expression. Say *What question could we ask about how Lily feels? How can we answer our question?* Guide children to realize that Lily is frustrated because the shop doesn't have any of the things she wants.

Pages 12–13 Ask *Does Josh have any food in his shop? What does he have?* Point out the word *hungry*. Guide children to break the word into syllables by counting the number of vowel sounds.

Pages 14–15 Ask *Why can't Lily's baby have an ice cream bar? Who eats it instead? How do you think Lily feels about Josh's shop now?*

Page 16 Ask *Do you think this is a good ending for the story? Why or why not?* Have children share questions they had about the story and discuss where they found the answers. Ask *How did asking and answering these questions help you understand the story better?*

Independent Practice

To further support application of the comprehension skill, have children reread the book using the Questions and Answers Chart for support. Assist children in filling in the chart with questions and finding answers as appropriate from the text and illustrations. Observe children as they read. Make note of how each child is or is not using the skills and strategies being focused on in this lesson.

3 Review

Reading Vocabulary

- Provide children with a copy of the Word Sorter. Write *Food* in the box at the top; write *Sweet* and *Not Sweet* in the second-tier boxes. Work with children to pick out the food words and sort them into these categories. Discuss key features of each food, such as things you can make with it or how you eat it.
- Have children highlight or add the reading vocabulary words in their copies of *My PM Word Book*. Encourage children to use these words in their writing.

Phonics

Write *inside* on chart paper. Recall with children how to count vowel sounds in a word to tell how many syllables it has. Repeat with *baby, igloo,* and *hunted*.

Fluency

Remind children to let their voices rise at the end when they read a question. Have them practice by reading the question on page 8.

Comprehension

Ask children to refer to their completed Questions and Answers Chart for *Josh's Shop* as you lead a discussion about the questions and answers that were recorded.

Writing Connection

- Tell children they will write a story about visiting Josh's shop. Ask them to think about what might happen if they went to Josh's shop. Suggest that children first draw a picture about what happens. Provide the following sentence stems to help them write their story:

  When I went to Josh's shop, _____ .

  Then I _____ .

  Josh _____ .

  In the end, _____ .

- Tell children that it is important to end a story in a way that makes it feel finished. Point out that telling what happened in the end, as the last sentence frame does, can help do this. Check that children's closing sentences give the story a sense of closure.

4 Assessment

Phonics

Have each child read the following two-syllable words using knowledge of consonant-vowel and consonant-vowel-consonant syllable patterns to decode: *hobby, pinto, misty, fancy*.

Fluency

Ask each child to read pages 6 and 8 aloud. Listen to make sure that their voices rise at the end of a question.

Comprehension

Review each child's Questions and Answers Chart, prompting the child to explain the comprehension strategy and to talk through the graphic organizer.

Differentiated Instruction

- **Auditory** learners can "hear" the story by listening to Lily's and Josh's words being read aloud by two classmates.
- **Kinesthetic** learners can "feel" the story by setting up a shop like Josh's that doesn't have some items.
- **Visual** learners can "see" the story by drawing the items Josh's shop does and doesn't have.

Character Spotlight

Lily

Tell children they may remember the character Lily from another book they have read. Ask a volunteer to name another book in which this character has appeared (*Lily's Apple*, Red Level). With children, use this book for comparison. Guide children to tell how Lily is the same and different between *Lily's Apple* and *Josh's Shop*. Record their responses in a Venn diagram.

Yellow **Level 6**

Name_____

Word Sorter

12

Josh's Shop PM Stars Teacher's Guide—Yellow Level

© Houghton Mifflin Harcourt. All rights reserved.

Name _____

Questions and Answers Chart

Title _____

Questions	Answers

Sit Down, Socks!

Written by Sally Cowan   Illustrated by Anne Spudvilas

Overview Rosa wants to take her cat, Socks, for a ride in her stroller. Socks does not seem to like the idea. What happens after he climbs up a tree?

Reading Vocabulary Words ride p. 2, doll p. 2, stroller p. 2, ladder p. 10, garage p. 12

Phonics Skill Long vowel *e*

Fluency Point Matching character's tone

Comprehension Strategy Using illustrations and details to describe

Reading Strategy Using punctuation as you read

Writing Connection Narrative

Common Core State Standards RL.1.2 Retell stories, including key details, and demonstrate understanding of their central message or lesson; RF.1.3c Know final -e and common vowel team conventions for representing long vowel sounds; RF.1.4b Read on-level text orally with accuracy, appropriate rate, and expression on successive readings; W.1.3 Write narratives in which they recount two or more appropriately sequenced events, include some details regarding what happened, use temporal words to signal event order, and provide some sense of closure.

Reading Word Count: 137

High-Frequency Words

this	stay
will	back
like	help

More books within the character series

Where Is Socks?
PM Stars Red Level 5

Go Away, Socks!
PM Stars Blue Level 9

1 Before Reading

Build Background

- Read aloud the title with children. Point out the author's and illustrator's names, talk about the cover illustrations, and share the overview. Say *Rosa wants her cat Socks to ride in her stroller.* Invite children to make predictions about what Socks does.

- Have children tell what they know about pets. Say *What kind of animals make good pets? How do you care for a pet? Do pets act like people?*

Focus on Reading Vocabulary

- Write each vocabulary word on chart paper, reading each aloud as you write it. Ask children to use the words to answer these questions: *Which word describes what you do on a bike? Which names a toy you can hug? Which is a thing in which to carry a baby? What might firefighters use to get to the top of a building? In what kind of building do cars park?*

- Model filling in a Word Web graphic organizer. Write *ride* in the center. With children's help, fill in the surrounding boxes with phrases that are related to the word. Encourage children to talk about the connections with a partner.

Focus on Phonics

Write *tree* on chart paper. Say the word aloud slowly. Explain *Tree has the long vowel ē at the end. Let's read this word slowly, making each of the sounds in it. In this story, we will see different ways to spell the long ē sound, such as: e as in we, ea as in please, and ee as in tree.* Continue with *cheese, team, me, he,* and *sleep*.

Focus on Fluency

Write *Cora smiled and said, "That joke is so funny!"* on chart paper. Point to the words as you read them with expression. Say *When I read, my tone was happy because the character was happy. I thought about how the character feels and read with the correct expression. I don't read every text in the same way.* Provide other sentences that express other emotions and read them chorally.

Focus on Comprehension

- Explain that readers can use illustrations and details in a book to learn about story characters and events. Details can give clues to how characters feel so readers can match the characters' tone and understand the story.
- Say *Writers often include many details in their writing. In stories, writers may give details to describe characters, setting, or events. Often, the illustrations provide additional details that are not written on the page.* Show a familiar fiction text as you use the illustrations and details from the text to describe the setting, the emotions of a character, and an event. Explain that the illustrations may show details about the characters or important scenes from the story.

2 Reading the Text

Have children read *Sit Down, Socks!* As appropriate, monitor application of the comprehension strategy and support strategic reading using the prompts below.

Pages 2–3 Ask *What does Rosa want? Describe how she is getting what she wants.*

Pages 4–5 Say *Think about how Rosa feels and how she sounds. How should you read to match Rosa's tone? Match her tone as you reread what she says.*

Pages 6–7 Focus children's attention on Socks. Say *Describe what Socks does. How far away do you think he runs? Use the illustration to help you decide..*

Pages 8–9 Point out that, in the text, Rosa cries for Mom's help. Ask *How does Rosa ask for help?* Point out the word *Please*. Ask *What vowel sound does this word have? How is the long e sound spelled?*

Pages 10–11 Ask *What is happening now in the story? In your answer, include details about what Rosa and Socks are doing.*

ESL/ELL

Some students might be confused by the *-er* endings of *ladder* and *stroller*, thinking that the words refer to a person. Explain that some words do not follow familiar spelling patterns. Say *For some words it's best to memorize them.* Suggest that children put these words in their copies of *My PM Word Book*.

Reading Strategy

Explain to children that they should attend to punctuation as they read. Ask them to point out punctuation on page 6. Remind them of the purpose for each mark. Explain that they should read words in quotations like the character who is speaking, pause at commas, stop reading when they come to a period, and read sentences ending with an exclamation point with appropriate expression.

High-Frequency Words

For children who need additional practice, use the appropriate cards from the *PM High-Frequency Word Cards* boxed set. Have children display the word cards one at a time like flash cards for their partner to read.

Visual Literacy

Have children study the scene depicted on page 3. Ask *Do Rosa and her Mom look happy or sad? Does Socks look happy or sad? How do you know?*

Pages 12–13 Say *How does Rosa try to get Socks to go to her? What does she say? What does she do? Use details from the text and illustration.*

Pages 14–15 Say *Look at Rosa. Look at Socks. Describe what they are doing and how you think they feel.*

Page 16 Say *How do you think Rosa feels? How do you think she is talking to Socks?*

Independent Practice

To further support application of the comprehensions strategy, have children reread the book using the Using Words and Pictures graphic organizer for support. Have children record details about one character as they read. Observe children as they read. Make note of how each child is or is not using the skills and strategies being focused on in this lesson.

3 Review

Reading Vocabulary

- Select a word, such as *ladder*, from this lesson's vocabulary list and model filling in the Word Web graphic organizer. Ask children to contribute ideas for other words and phrases that relate to the selected word.
- Have children highlight, or add, the reading vocabulary words in their copies of *My PM Word Book*. Encourage children to use these words in their writing.

Phonics

Write the following words from the book on chart paper. Have children identify the words with the long ē sound: *please, get, stay, tree, sit, not, sleep, my, went, she.*

Fluency

Have pairs of children take turns rereading pages 6 and 8, focusing on matching Rosa's tone.

Comprehension

Ask children to refer to their completed Using Words and Pictures graphic organizers for *Sit Down, Socks!* as you lead a discussion about key text and picture details about the characters.

Writing Connection

- Say *A narrative is a telling of events, like a story. Let's write a short narrative.* Brainstorm with children a recent occurrence they could write about.
- Explain that writers often retell events by writing about them in the order that they happened so that readers will not get confused. Add that they use time order words, such as *at first, after that,* and *finally*, to write things in order. Provide the following sentence stems for children:

  At first _____ .
  After that _____ .
  Finally _____ .

  Allow children not yet able to write sentences to draw pictures and label them *At first*, *After that*, and *Finally*.

4 Assessment

Phonics
Provide children a familiar book that has words with the long vowel *e* to reread. Check to make sure that children are reading the words correctly.

Fluency
Individually, have children read page 8 or 16 aloud. Check to make sure that children are matching the characters' tones.

Comprehension
Review each child's Using Words and Pictures graphic organizer, prompting each child to explain the comprehension strategy and to talk through the organizer.

Differentiated Instruction

- **Kinesthetic** learners can "feel" the words by acting out putting a stuffed toy into a toy stroller.
- **Auditory** learners can "hear" the words by working with partners and listening as one partner reads the text.
- **Visual** learners can "see" the words by looking at pictures of people showing the same feelings as Rosa on their face.

Character Spotlight

Socks

Explain to children that books follow a sequence of events. If one of the events were to change, it would change the character's actions. Have children brainstorm what they think might happen if Rosa put Socks back in the stroller. Have them describe how Socks would feel and what the cat might do.

Yellow **Level 7** 17

Name_____

Word Web

Sit Down, Socks! PM Stars Teacher's Guide—Yellow Level

Name _____

Using Words and Pictures

page	What the words say	What the picture shows

Sit Down, Socks! PM Stars Teacher's Guide—Yellow Level

Jet Is Naughty

Written by Annette Smith   Illustrated by Richard Hoit

Overview Harry wants to go to the park. Mom says he must clean up his room first. Jet decides to help. What will Jet do?

Reading Vocabulary Words park p. 3, bedroom p. 5, shoes p. 9, school p. 9, cried p. 11, naughty p. 11, helicopter p. 13, box p. 15

Vocabulary Skill Shades of meaning

Phonics Skill Spelling pattern *CVVC*

Fluency Point Using loudness and softness to express emotion

Comprehension Strategy Using illustrations and details to describe

Reading Strategy Pointing to each word as you read

Writing Connection Story

Common Core State Standards RL.1.7 Use illustrations and details in a story to describe its characters, setting, or events; RF.1.3b Decode regularly spelled one-syllable words; RF.1.4b Read grade-level text orally with accuracy, appropriate rate, and expression; W.1.3 Write narratives in which they recount two or more appropriately sequenced events, include some details regarding what happened, use temporal words to signal event order, and provide some sense of closure; L.1.5d Distinguish shades of meaning among verbs differing in manner and adjectives differing in intensity by defining or choosing them or by acting out the meanings.

Reading Word Count: 134

High-Frequency Words

today	back
your	with
will	came

More books within the character series

Harry and the Little Robot
PM Stars Red Level 3

Jet, the Little Robot
PM Stars Red Level 5

1 Before Reading

Build Background

- Introduce the book by reading the title aloud with children. Point out the author's and illustrator's names. Explain that someone who is naughty has done something they shouldn't have. Ask *Does Jet look naughty in this picture? Why do you think that? How might a robot be naughty?* Invite children to point out details and make predictions.
- Have children tell about having to clean their rooms. Ask *How messy is your room? Do you clean your room on your own or does someone have to remind you? Do you have to clean your room before you can do other things?*

Focus on Reading Vocabulary

- Write each Reading Vocabulary word on a piece of chart paper, leaving a space below it. Read each word aloud and ask children to tell what they know about it. If needed, explain that a helicopter is a kind of flying machine. As a class draw or find a picture that represents each word and paste it to the chart paper below the word. Have children use each word in a sentence.

- Tell children that some words mean almost the same thing, but every word is just a little different from other words. Say *Some words are stronger or weaker than other words. Some word tell about actions that are almost alike but are done a little differently.* Ask volunteers to act out *look, peek,* and *stare.* Ask *How are these ways of looking different?* Then discuss the difference between *big, huge,* and *gigantic.* Ask *Which word is the strongest? Which is the weakest?*
- Model filling in a Word Wheel. Write *cried* in the middle. Have children suggest words that mean about the same as *cried* but are done a little differently. Write these words around the outside of the wheel.

Focus on Phonics

Write *stood* on chart paper and say it aloud slowly. Repeat the word, pointing out the *oo* sound. Say *This word uses the spelling pattern consonant-vowel-vowel-consonant (CVVC). When words use this spelling pattern, the vowels usually work together to make one sound. The letters* oo *can make the short* oo *sound in* book *or the long* oo *sound in* cool. Repeat with *town*, pointing out that *w* is usually a consonant, but it acts as a vowel in this combination to make the /ow/ sound.

Focus on Fluency

Tell children that good readers make their voices louder or softer to show what a character is feeling. Say *When you read, look for clues in the text that tell what the character is feeling. Then make your voice louder or softer to match that feeling.* Ask *If a character is excited, should I read her words louder or softer? If a character is afraid, how should I read his words?*

Focus on Comprehension

Say *Remember, looking at the pictures in books can tell you more about the people, places, and events in the story. Good readers look at the pictures as well as read the text to understand what is happening in the story.* Choose a person, place, or event from a familiar classroom picture book and use details from both the text and the pictures to describe it.

2 Reading the Text

Have children read *Jet Is Naughty*. As appropriate, monitor application of the comprehension strategy and support strategic reading using the prompts below.

Pages 2–3 Ask *How would you describe Harry's bedroom?* Have children use picture details to answer the question. Point to the word *down*. Ask *What spelling pattern do you see in this word? What sound do the letters* ow *make?* Say the word together.

Pages 4–5 Say *Mom tells Harry to look at his room. Can you tell what she means from the picture? Look at her finger. Look at Harry's face. What is Mom telling Harry to do?*

ESL/ELL

Work with children to brainstorm words that indicate the reader should use loudness or softness when reading. Allow children to act out the words if they do not know them. Help children sort the words into the categories *Loud* and *Soft*. Children can refer to this chart as they read other books.

Reading Strategy

Explain to children that when there are a lot of words on a page, it's easy to lose your place. Say *If you point to each word as you read it, you won't skip words, and you'll always know where you are on the page.* Have children practice by reading page 9, pointing to each word as they read it.

High-Frequency Words

For children who need additional practice, use the appropriate cards from the *PM High-Frequency Word* Cards boxed set. Have children choose two words and use them in a sentence.

Visual Literacy

Have children look at the picture of Harry on page 4. Ask *Does Harry look happy or unhappy? How can you tell?* Have children redraw Harry, changing his facial expression to represent his different emotions as the book unfolds.

Pages 6–7 Have children refer to the pictures to answer the questions *What is Harry asking Jet to help him with? How does Jet answer him? If Jet could talk, what do you think he would say?*

Pages 8–9 Ask *What is Harry doing? Why is he telling Jet where things go?* Point to *school* and have children identify the spelling pattern it uses. Remind them of the two sounds *oo* makes. Have them try both and tell which one makes a word.

Pages 10–11 Ask *Why is* naughty *a good word for what Jet is doing?* Then ask *What clues show how Harry feels?* Guide children to identify *cried*, exclamation points, and Harry's expression. Model reading Harry's words more loudly to show that he is angry.

Pages 12–13 Say *Use details from the picture to tell what Jet does with Harry's hat.* Point to the vocabulary word *helicopter*. Ask *How are Jet and a helicopter alike?*

Pages 14–15 Say *Harry wants Jet to get back in his box. Why do you think this is?*

Page 16 Say *Look at the picture of Harry's bedroom now. Why do you think Mom changed her mind about going to the park?* Discuss with children how using details from the pictures to describe people, places, and events in the story helped them understand the story.

Individual Reading

To further support application of the comprehension skill, have children reread the book using the Using Words and Pictures graphic organizer for support. Assist children in filling in the chart with details about the people, places, and events in the story. Observe children as they read. Make note of how each child is or is not using the skills and strategies being focused on in this lesson.

 3 Review

Reading Vocabulary

- Provide children with a copy of the Word Wheel. Write *naughty* in the center oval. Ask children to suggest words that are similar in meaning to *naughty* but are stronger or weaker. Record responses in the outer ring of the wheel.
- Have children highlight, or add, the reading vocabulary words in their copies of *My PM Word Book*. Encourage children to use these words in their writing.

Phonics

Write *good*, *food*, and *frown* on the board. Have children read the words. Ask volunteers to explain what spelling pattern they use and what sound each vowel pair makes. Have children name other words that use the same spelling pattern.

Fluency

Have children take turns reading page 11 aloud. Remind them to change the volume of their voices, remembering to read louder or softer when they want to show emotion.

Comprehension

Ask children to refer to their completed Using Words and Pictures graphic organizer for *Jet Is Naughty* as you lead a discussion about the questions and answers that were recorded.

Writing Connection

- Tell children they will make up a story about how Jet "helps" Harry do something else. As a class, brainstorm a list of other tasks Harry might have to do. Ask children to choose a task and think about how Jet might "help" Harry get it done.
- Remind children stories should tell what happened in order. Good writers use order words to show when things happened. Have children write their stories using the following sentence stems to show order:

  First _____.
  Then _____.
  Next _____.
  Finally _____.

4 Assessment

Phonics

Write *brown, book, school, hood, town,* and *tool* on the board. Point to each word and have children read it aloud.

Fluency

Have individual children read page 15 aloud. Check to see if they are changing the loudness and softness of their voices as characters' emotions change.

Comprehension

Review each child's Using Words and Pictures graphic organizer, prompting the child to explain the comprehension strategy and to talk through the organizer.

Differentiated Instruction

- **Kinesthetic** learners can "feel" the story by acting out what Harry, his mom, and Jet do in the story.
- **Auditory** learners can "hear" the story by listening to an adult read it aloud as they follow along.
- **Visual** learners can "see" the story by drawing pictures that show Harry's room in the beginning, middle, and end of the story.

Character Spotlight

Jet

Explain to children that characters in stories have unique features that make them special. One thing that makes them special is their physical traits, or what they look like. Have children write a description of what Jet looks like.

Name_____

Word Wheel

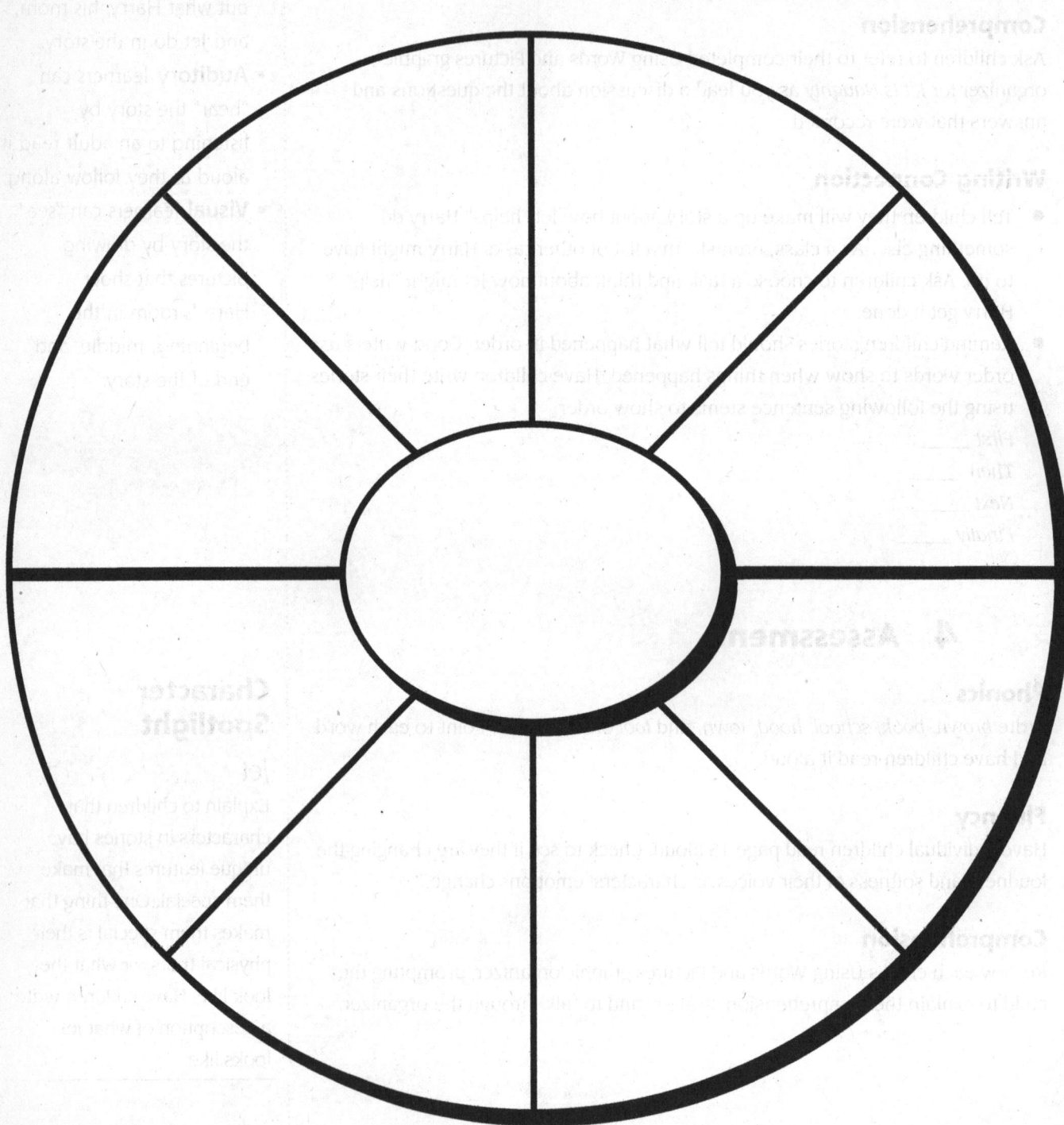

Name_____

Using Words and Pictures

page	What the words say	What the picture shows

Jet Is Naughty PM Stars Teacher's Guide—Yellow Level

Pokey Is Sick

Written by Debbie Croft Illustrated by Debbie Mourtzios

Overview Tess thinks that her dog, Pokey, is sick. Her brother, Danny, thinks that he can help. What can Danny do to help?

Reading Vocabulary Words kitchen p. 3, puppy p. 3, sick p. 3, basket p. 5, yard p. 9, cold p. 15, wet p. 15

Vocabulary Skill Context clues

Phonics Skill Multiple-syllable words

Fluency Point Matching character's voice

Comprehension Strategy Retelling story events or key details

Reading Strategy Using punctuation as you read

Writing Connection Story

Common Core State Standards RL.1.4a Identify words and phrases in stories or poems that suggest feelings or appeal to the senses; RF.1.3e Decode two-syllable words following basic patterns by breaking the words into syllables; RF.1.4b Read on-level text orally with accuracy, appropriate rate, and expression on successive readings; W.1.3 Write narratives in which they recount two or more appropriately sequenced events, include some details regarding what happened, use temporal words to signal event order, and provide some sense of closure; L.1.4a Use sentence-level context as a clue to the meaning of a word or phrase.

Reading Word Count: 150

High-Frequency Words

got	came
out	I'm
of	outside

More books within the character series

Pokey and the Slipper
PM Stars Blue Level 9

The Birthday Boy
PM Green Level 12

Grandpa's Visit
PM Stars Green Level 12

1 Before Reading

Build Background

- Read aloud the title with children. Point out the author's and illustrator's names, talk about the cover illustration, and share the overview. Invite children to make predictions about what Tess does and how Pokey feels.
- Have children tell what they know about being sick. Ask *How did you feel? What did you want to do when you were sick?*

Focus on Reading Vocabulary

- Write each vocabulary word, reading aloud as you write. Have children answer these questions: *Where do you cook food? What is "a baby dog"? What is the opposite of healthy? What is used to hold or carry things? What grassy area is around a house? What is the opposite of hot? What is the opposite of dry?*
- Explain that the other words in a sentence can be context clues. They can help readers figure out the meaning of unknown words. They can give readers an idea of the word's meaning.
- Model filling in a Context Clues graphic organizer. Write *We often eat breakfast in the kitchen* on chart paper and *kitchen* in the top box of the organizer. Work with children to select the other words in the sentence that help you know the meaning of *kitchen* and to decide what the word means.

Focus on Phonics

Say *One way to decode a long word is to study its into syllables. Look for familiar spelling patterns in the word's syllables.* Write *kit chen* on chart paper, leaving a space between the syllables. Point out the consonant-vowel-consonant spelling pattern in each syllable. Have children pronounce the syllables and read the word. Repeat with *basket* and *puppy*.

Focus on Fluency

Explain that it is important to change your voice when reading what a story character says and what the narrator says. Say *Details in the story signal how to read what a character or the narrator say.* Write the following sentences on chart paper: *The dog ran away from Kim. "Come back, Noodle!" yelled Kim.* Model using the details that the dog ran away and Kim yelled to decide how to read the sentences. Then change your voice between the narration and character speech.

Focus on Comprehension

Say *Just as things happen in real life, story events happen in order. You can use their order to retell the story.* Recall with children the beginning, middle, and end of a familiar fiction book. Ask them to help you fill in the Retelling Chart graphic organizer by retelling the story events in order.

2 Reading the Text

Have children read *Pokey Is Sick*. As appropriate, monitor application of the comprehension strategy and support strategic reading using the prompts below.

Pages 2–3 Ask children to identify the characters and setting of the story. Discuss Tess's voice with children. Ask *How do you think Tess says Pokey's name? How does her voice sound when she says the other sentences?*

Pages 4–5 Ask *What happens next?* Focus children's attention on Tess. *What does Pokey do after Tess gets water?* Point out the last sentence. Ask *What words in this sentence are clues to the meaning of* basket*?*

Pages 6–7 Have children identify the new character. Ask *What happens in the story now? What is Pokey doing?*

Pages 8–9 Have children retell the beginning of the story. Ask *What has happened so far in the story?* Point out the word *Danny*. Ask *How many syllables does* Danny *have? What spelling pattern does each syllable have? How can you read this long word?*

ESL/ELL

Provide additional practice with the meaning and use of English punctuation marks. While working with children throughout the day, point out punctuation that appears in any texts, title, and headings.

Reading Strategy

Explain that punctuation like commas and periods that signal a pause, exclamation points, and question marks are clues to how text should be read. Have children locate a comma, period, exclamation mark, question mark, and quotation mark within the text. Ask children to read the sentence using the punctuation, and then explain the purpose of each mark.

High-Frequency Words

For children who need additional practice, use the appropriate cards from the *PM High-Frequency Word Cards* boxed set. Have partners place the word cards facedown and take turns choosing one at random and reading the word.

Visual Literacy

Have children look at the picture of Tess on page 8. *Is Tess happy or worried? How can you tell?* Have children find another picture of Tess that shows the other feeling.

Pages 10–11 Explain that on these pages Tess, Danny, and Pokey don't *do* anything. Instead, Tess and Danny have a conversation. Ask *Why do you think the author writes this conversation?*

Pages 12–13 Point out that sometimes story events are the things that characters do. Ask *What does Danny do? What two things does Pokey do? When does she get out of her basket?*

Pages 14–15 Ask *How did Danny know that Pokey was not sick? How do you think his voice sounds?* Point out the words *cold* and *wet*. Have children name other things that are cold and wet.

Page 16 How does the ending of the story leave the reader feeling? Have children retell the beginning, middle, and end of the story in only three sentences.

Independent Practice

To further support application of the comprehension strategy, have children reread the book using the Retelling Chart graphic organizer for support. Have children select a pairing of illustration and text to represent the beginning, the middle, and the end of the story. Observe children as they read. Note how each child is or is not using the skills and strategies being focused on in this lesson.

3 Review

Reading Vocabulary

- Select a word, such as *yard*, from this lesson's vocabulary list and model filling in the Context Clues graphic organizer. Ask children to contribute their ideas for words and phrases that help them understand the word's meaning.
- Have children highlight, or add, the reading vocabulary words in their copies of *My PM Word Book*. Encourage children to use these words in their writing.

Phonics

Have children decode the following multiple-syllable story words: *rocket, coffee, explode*. Discuss the spelling patterns by writing each word with a space between the syllables. Ask children to read the word and then identify the spelling pattern of each syllable.

Fluency

With a partner, have children take turns reading page 11 aloud, thinking about how the character feels and matching the character's voice.

Comprehension

Ask children to refer to their completed Retelling Chart graphic organizers for *Pokey Is Sick* as you lead a discussion about the story, including key events.

Writing Connection

- Say *A story is a telling of something real or made up that happened. Stories have characters who do things and events that happen in order. Let's imagine and write a story about a boy and his pet.* Brainstorm with children a human character and a pet for the title of the their stories. Have children think about a beginning, middle, and end for their story. Provide the following sentence frames to guide children's writing:

  _____ had a pet.
  It was a _____.
  At first, it _____.
  Then one day, it _____.
  In the end, _____.

- Explain that authors use time order words, such as *at first, then,* or *in the end,* to write things in order so that readers will not get confused. Allow children not yet ready to write complete sentences to draw and label pictures of a beginning, middle, and end of a story.

4 Assessment

Phonics
Have children reread a familiar book and find words with multiple syllables to decode on their own using spelling patterns.

Fluency
Individually, have children read page 15 aloud. Check to make sure that children are matching the character's voice.

Comprehension
Review each child's Retelling Chart graphic organizer, prompting each child to explain the comprehension strategy and to talk through the graphic organizer.

Differentiated Instruction

- **Tactile** learners can "feel" the words by touching items that feel the same way as a puppy, such as cotton balls or felt.
- **Auditory** learners can "hear" the words by working with partners and listening as one partner reads the text.
- **Visual** learners can "see" the words by looking at pictures of people showing their feelings in different their facial expressions.

Character Spotlight

Have children think about the characters Tess and Danny in the book and what was the same and different between them. Provide them with two pieces of paper. Have them write characteristics of Tess on one page and Danny on the other.

Yellow **Level 8** 29

Name_____

Context Clues

word I don't know

↓

words that help me understand

↓

word's meaning

Name _____

Retelling Chart

Title _____

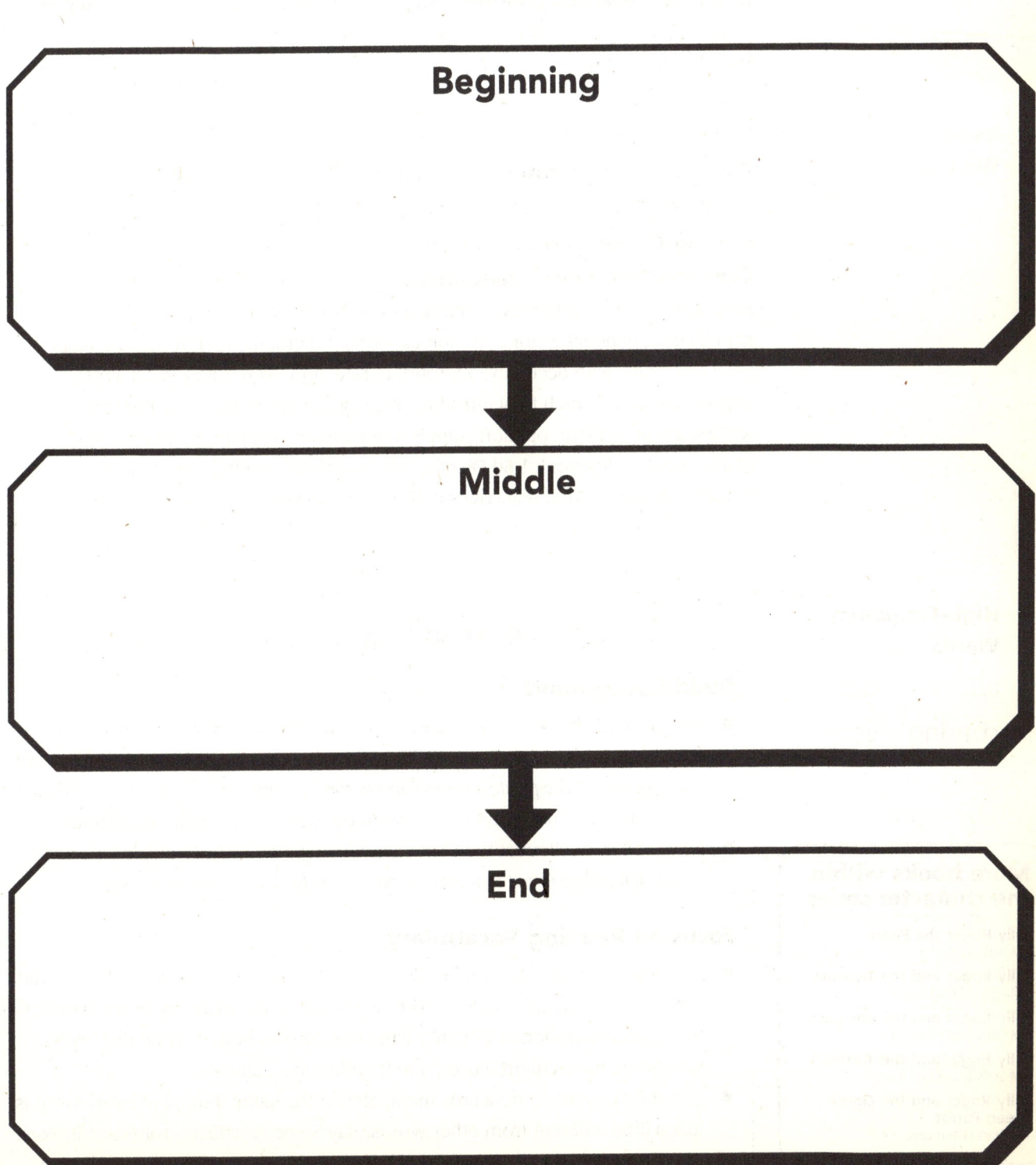

Pokey Is Sick PM Stars Teacher's Guide—Yellow Level 8

Jolly Roger and the Coconuts

Written by Elsie Nelley Illustrated by Chantal Stewart

Overview Jolly Roger and the pirates want to eat coconuts. Coconuts are hard to get. The pirates can't reach the coconuts. Can Jolly Roger get the coconuts?

Reading Vocabulary Words fish p. 2, coconuts p. 2, safe p. 6, shouted p. 8, coat p. 10, boots p. 10, dirty p. 10, waves p. 14

Vocabulary Skill Shades of meaning

Phonics Skill Consonant digraph *sh*

Fluency Point Matching character's feelings and emotions

Comprehension Strategy Comparing and contrasting information

Reading Strategy Looking at the picture and at the word's first letter

Writing Connection Book review

Common Core State Standards RL.1.9 Compare and contrast the adventures and experiences of characters in stories; RF.1.3a Know the spelling-sound correspondences for common consonant digraphs; RF.1.4b Read grade-level text orally with accuracy, appropriate rate, and expression; W.1.1 Write opinion pieces in which they introduce the topic or name the book they are writing about, state an opinion, supply a reason for the opinion, and provide some sense of closure; L.1.5d Distinguish shades of meaning among verbs differing in manner and adjectives differing in intensity by defining or choosing them or by acting out the meanings.

Reading Word Count: 150

High-Frequency Words

all   out
coming   very

More books within the character series

Jolly Roger the Pirate
PM Yellow Level 6

Jolly Roger and the Treasure
PM Plus Yellow Level 7

Jolly Roger and the Spyglass
PM Stars Blue Level 11

Jolly Roger and the Turtles
PM Stars Blue Level 11

Jolly Roger and the Clever Green Parrot
PM Stars Green Level 14

 ## 1 Before Reading

Build Background

- Introduce the book by reading the title with children. Point out the author's and illustrator's name. Point to the coconuts and say *Coconuts are good to eat. Jolly Roger and the pirates are looking at the coconuts on the tree. How will they get them down?* Invite children to point out details and make predictions.
- Have children tell what they know about coconuts. Ask *Where do coconuts grow? What do you eat that has coconut in it? How does coconut taste?*

Focus on Reading Vocabulary

- Write each Reading Vocabulary word on a blank card. Hold up each card and read the word aloud. Guide children to point out the meaning of the word in the cover illustration and/or tell what they know about it. Then display two words and have children use them together in a sentence.
- Tell children that some words mean almost the same thing, but every word is just a little different from other words. Say *Some describing words are stronger or weaker than others. Some action words are done a just little differently.* Act out *walk, skip,* and *jog.* Ask *How these ways of moving different?* Then discuss the difference between *little, small,* and *tiny.* Ask *Which word is the strongest? Which is the weakest?*

- Display the Word Wheel graphic organizer and model filling it in. Write *shouted* in the center circle. Brainstorm words for ways of vocalizing, such as *said*, *whispered*, *cried*, *yelled*, *sang*, and *growled*. Record words in the outside ring of the wheel.

Focus on Phonics

Write the word *shore* on chart paper. Say the word slowly, and then repeat the word, stressing the /sh/ sound. Point to the letters *sh* and say *These two letters work together to make one sound, /sh/. This is called a digraph.* Have children identify the *sh* digraph in the words *ship* and *wash* and then say the words.

Focus on Fluency

Explain that good readers think about how a character is feeling when they read his or her words. On the board, write a line of dialogue from a favorite fiction book that shows a character's emotion. Ask children to follow along as you read the sentence aloud. Say *When you read the words that a character says, try to show how that character feels.* Read the sentence, mimicking how the character would say the line. Then invite children to read the sentence chorally with you.

Focus on Comprehension

Explain to children that comparing and contrasting the experiences of characters helps them notice similarities and differences between stories. Say *When we compare two characters, we look for ways they are alike. When we contrast two characters, we look for ways they are different.* Draw a simple Compare and Contrast graphic organizer on the board. Model the skill by examining the experiences of two main characters in familiar fiction stories using the organizer.

ESL/ELL

Write *hungry*, *cried*, *shouted*, *not safe*, and *thanks* on the board. Pair English language learners with more proficient speakers. Have the pairs work together to find pictures in the book that show the emotion being described by each word or phrase.

2 Reading the Text

Have children read *Jolly Roger and the Coconuts*. Select a recently read fiction book to use with the prompts below. As appropriate, monitor application of the comprehension strategy and support strategic reading using these prompts.

Pages 2–3 Say *Little Pirate and Big Pirate are trying to catch fish. Is it working? What do the pirates need or want?* Discuss with children how the beginning of the story is the same as or different from the recently read fiction book you are using with Reading the Text.

Pages 4–5 Point to the vocabulary word *coconuts*. Ask *What are coconuts? How are they the same as and different from fish? Where do you see coconuts? Do you think Little Pirate will be able to get them? Why or why not?*

Pages 6–7 Point out the first sentence. Ask *What does Little Pirate say? What word in the text tells you how he says it? What does the word* safe *mean? How does Little Pirate feel?* Have a volunteer read the first sentence, using expression to show Little Pirate's feelings.

Reading Strategy

Say *If you come to a word you don't know, you can say the sound of the first letter and then look for something in the picture that starts with that sound.* Point to *boots* on page 10. Ask *What is the first letter in this word? What sound does it make?* Have children find something of Jolly Roger's in the illustration that starts with a *b* sound.

High-Frequency Words

For children who need additional practice, use the appropriate cards from the *PM High-Frequency Word Cards* boxed set. Pair children. Have one child read each word and the other child write it on a blank card. Have children take turns in the roles until all the cards match.

Visual Literacy

Have children look at the pictures of Little Pirate on pages 11 and 15. Ask them to tell how they think he feels on each page. Encourage them to give reasons to support their choice of words.

Pages 8–9 Ask *Why can't Little Pirate get the coconuts? Why can't Big Pirate get the coconuts?* Guide children in a discussion analyzing how Little Pirate's experience is the same as and different from the main character in the other fiction text chosen for this reading?

Pages 10–11 Ask *Why doesn't Jolly Roger want to get the coconuts?* Invite children to suggest solutions to the problem.

Pages 12–13 Point out how Big Pirate and Little Pirate offer to help. Compare and contrast this with how characters in the other fiction story work to solve a problem. Ask *Do you think Jolly Roger will be able to get the coconuts now? Why or why not?*

Pages 14–15 Ask *Why do you think Jolly Roger was able to get the coconuts?* Have children identify the words with the *sh* digraph on this page (*shouted, Splash*). Call on volunteers to read the words.

Page 16 Ask *Did the pirates get what they needed at the beginning of the story? How do you know?* Discuss with children how comparing and contrasting characters' experiences makes them better readers.

Individual Reading

To further support application of the comprehension skill, have children reread the book using the Compare and Contrast graphic organizer for support. Assist children in filling in the organizer with details that tell how Jolly Roger's and the pirates' experiences were the same as and different from the experiences of character's in a familiar fiction text. Observe children as they read. Make note of how each child is or is not using the skill being focused on in this lesson.

 3 Review

Reading Vocabulary

- Provide children with a copy of the Word Wheel. Write *dirty* in the center circle. Working with children, write words that mean about the same but are stronger or weaker, such as *dusty, grimy,* and *filthy*.
- Have children highlight, or add, the reading vocabulary words in their copies of *My PM Word Book*. Encourage children to use these words in their writing.

Phonics

Write *fish* and *ship* on the chalkboard. Say the words aloud and have children identify the /sh/ sound. Remind children that the letters *sh* work together make the sound /sh/. Brainstorm other words from the story illustrations that use the consonant digraph *sh*, such as *shirt, shoe,* and *shore,* and list them on the board.

Fluency

Remind children that when they read the words said by a character, they should try to show how the character feels. Have children read page 8 in a way that reflects how Big Pirate feels.

Comprehension

Ask children to refer to their completed Compare and Contrast organizer for *Jolly Roger and the Coconuts* as you lead a discussion about the similarities and differences that were recorded.

Writing Connection

- Tell children that they will be writing a book review. Say *Remember, a book review tells your opinion of a book you have read*. Write the following sentence stems on the board to help children write their book review:

  I read _____ .

  I _____ the book.

  I _____ it because _____ .

  You _____ read this book.

- Say *Good writers tell readers their opinion. They also give reasons for their opinion. This tells readers why they should agree with the writer.* Tell children that the second sentence in their review tells their opinion and the third sentence gives the reason for their opinion. Point out that the word *because* is used to signal the reason for their opinion.

4 Assessment

Phonics

Have each child find and read two or more words from the book that contain the consonant digraph *sh*.

Fluency

Individually, have children read page 12 aloud. Observe to make sure that each child's reading reflects how Little Pirate feels in this scene.

Comprehension

Review each child's Compare and Contrast organizer, prompting the child to explain the comprehension strategy and to talk through the graphic organizer.

Differentiated Instruction

- **Tactile** learners can "feel" the story by imagining what it feels like to climb a tall tree or recalling what it feels like to be hungry.
- **Auditory** learners can "hear" the story by listening to classmates read the character's words as they follow along.
- **Visual** learners can "see" the story by drawing the pirate's problem and its resolution.

Character Spotlight

Little Pirate and Big Pirate

Explain to children that characters, just like real people, are special in ways that make them different from other characters. Thinking about how two characters are alike and different makes stories more interesting. Have children tell how Little Pirate and Big Pirate are alike and how they differ from each other.

Name_____

Word Wheel

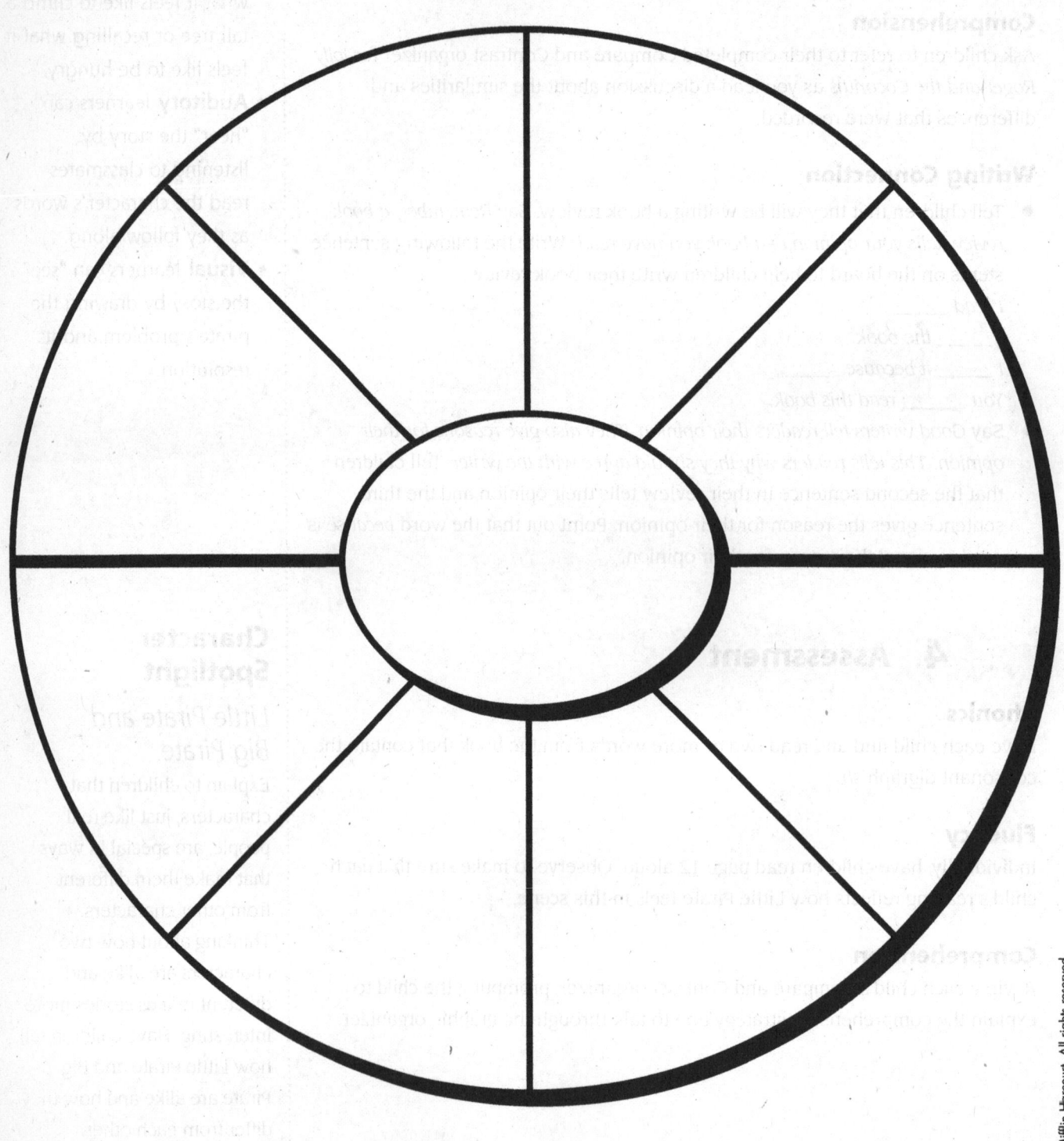

36 Jolly Roger and the Coconuts PM Stars Teacher's Guide—Yellow Level

Name _____

Compare and Contrast

Both

Jolly Roger and the Coconuts PM Stars Teacher's Guide—Yellow Level

The Town Garden

Written by Sally Cowan **Photographs by Lindsay Edwards**

Overview A boy and his mother visit the town garden. They see different plants and birds there. What do you think visitors do in a town garden?

Reading Vocabulary Words garden p. 2, town p. 2, flowers p. 4, plants p. 6, trees p. 8, birds, p. 10

Phonics Skill Spelling pattern *CV*

Fluency Point Reading smoothly

Comprehension Strategy Identifying topic and key details

Reading Strategy Looking at the picture and at the word's first letter

Writing Connection Explanation

Common Core State Standards RI.1.2 Identify the main topic and retell key details of a text; RF.1.3b Decode regularly spelled one-syllable words; RF.1.4b Read grade-level text orally with accuracy, appropriate rate, and expression; W.1.2 Write informative/explanatory texts in which they name a topic, supply some facts about the topic, and provide some sense of closure.

Reading Word Count: 144

High-Frequency Words

walk   some
day   they
it   good
like

More books within the leisure and work theme

Mailboxes
PM Stars Red Levels 5/6

The Big Ship
PM Stars Yellow Levels 8/9

Bird Watching on Vacation
PM Stars Blue Levels 11/12

Bike Safety
PM Stars Green Levels 14/15

 **1 Before Reading**

Build Background

- Read aloud the title with children. Point out the author's name. Say *These people must be going to a* town garden. *I wonder what people see and do at a town garden.* Invite children to point out details and make predictions.
- Have children tell what they know about a garden. Ask *Have you ever visited a garden in your town? Why do people visit gardens? What would you do the next time you visit a town garden?*

Focus on Reading Vocabulary

- Write each vocabulary word on chart paper, reading it aloud as you write it. Then ask children to read the words with you. To help children understand the relationship between the words, ask *What are some things you would see in a town garden?* Write children's responses on the board. Work together to underline the reading vocabulary words in their sentences.
- Model filling in a Word Web graphic organizer. Write the word *garden* in the center. Brainstorm with children words that describe a garden or name things that grow in or live in a garden, such as *beautiful, green, plants, flowers, butterflies, bees, birds,* and *trees*. Write some of these words in the boxes surrounding the center.

38 PM Stars Teacher's Guide

Focus on Phonics

Write *we* on the board. Have children clap as they say the word to count the number of syllables. Say *When a vowel comes after a consonant in a one-syllable word, you usually pronounce the vowel with a long sound.* Continue with the words *go, be,* and *by.*

Focus on Fluency

Read aloud a few sentences from a nonfiction book you read as a class. Have children follow along as you read. Point out that you read the sentences smoothly, without stopping or repeating words. Say *Reading smoothly does not mean reading fast. When I read smoothly, I understand the ideas on each page better.* Reread the sentences chorally with children.

Focus on Comprehension

Explain to children that nonfiction books are written to explore a topic. To identify the topic of a nonfiction book have children ask themselves "What is this book about?" Remind children that often the book title will tell the main topic of the book. Tell children that the author includes information to help readers understand the topic, and that the most important details about the topic are called *key details.* Explain that key details support the topic by telling *how, what, when, where, why, how much,* or *how many.*

2 Reading the Text

Have children read *The Town Garden*. As appropriate, monitor application of the comprehension strategy and support strategic reading using the prompts below.

Contents — Reread the title and point out that the topic of this book is a town garden. Have children look at the section headings in the Contents list. Ask *What kind of details about the town garden will we read on page 10?*

Pages 2–3 — Ask *Who is telling us about the town garden?* Point out the vocabulary word *town.* Ask children to tell what the word *town* means.

Pages 4–5 — Point out the heading and say *This section of the book is about plants in the town garden.* Ask *What types of plants are mentioned on page 4? (grass, flowers)* Say *Sometimes key details are given special attention on the page with boldface words and photographs.* Ask children to point to a word that ends with the long *i* sound and to explain the spelling pattern.

Pages 6–7 — Ask *What types of plants are mentioned on page 6? (big plants) What key detail has been given special attention in a photograph?*

ESL/ELL

After reading the book, review the vocabulary words and discuss what they mean. Then have children use the words to retell the information about town gardens from the book.

Reading Strategy

Explain to children that when they come to an unknown word when reading, looking at the picture and noticing the first letter of the word can help them. Model this strategy on page 6 of *The Town Garden.* Read aloud, stopping before *leaves.* Say *The picture shows a lot of leaves* and *the first letter of the unknown word is l.* Then reread the sentence to model self-monitoring for meaning.

Yellow **Levels 8/9** 39

High-Frequency Words

For children who need additional practice, use the appropriate cards from the *PM High-Frequency Word Cards* boxed set. Pair children and have them practice writing the high-frequency words.

Visual Literacy

Have children look at the photographs on page 4. Ask *What do you see in the large photograph on the page? What do you see in the small photograph at the bottom? What is the bee doing in that small photograph? How does this close-up photograph help you better understand the words?* Repeat with the photographs on page 6.

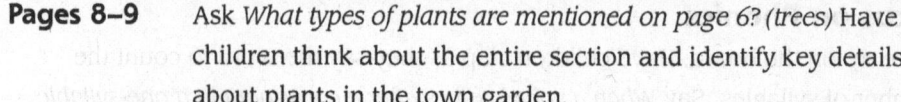

Pages 8–9   Ask *What types of plants are mentioned on page 6? (trees)* Have children think about the entire section and identify key details about plants in the town garden.

Pages 10–11   Ask *In this section, what do you learn about the town garden?* Remind children that the boldface word points out important information. Have children echo read the page with you to practice reading smoothly.

Pages 12–13   Say *Let's read the title of this section together. As you read, think about what the author wants you to know about a good day out.*

Pages 14–15   Have children turn back to the beginning of this section (page 12). Ask *What important information about a good day at the town garden do you learn in this section?*

Independent Practice

To further support application of the comprehension skill, have children reread the book using the Topic and Key Details graphic organizer for support. Assist children in filling in the topic of the book and prompt them to write or illustrate three key details from the book. Observe children as they read. Make note of how each child is or is not using the skills and strategies being focused on in this lesson.

 ## 3 Review

Reading Vocabulary

- Select a word, such as *bird*, from this lesson's vocabulary list and model filling in the Word Web graphic organizer. Ask children to contribute their ideas for other words that relate to the selected word.
- Have children highlight, or add, the reading vocabulary words in their copies of *My PM Word Book*. Encourage children to use these words in their writing.

Phonics

On chart paper write the word *me*. Review with children how to use what they know about reading a one-syllable word with a consonant followed by one vowel to decode. Have children practice using this skill to read the following words: *he, she, no, so, hi*.

Fluency

Have individual children read page 4 aloud. Discuss with children the qualities of reading smoothly.

Comprehension

Ask children to refer to their completed Topic and Key Details graphic organizers for *The Town Garden* as you lead a discussion about the recorded details.

Writing Connection

- Explain to children that they will write an explanation telling about a visit to a place in the community with their class or family. Brainstorm with children for ideas. Have children use the name of the place chosen as the title of their explanation. Write and discuss the following directions on the board:
Write the title.
Where did you go?
Why did you go there?
Tell one fact about the visit.
Did you enjoy the visit?

- Tell children that the sentences in their explanation will include facts and details about the visit. Assist children in writing facts that are key to their topics.

4 Assessment

Phonics

On index cards, write *so, be, my, no,* and *me*. Have each child pronounce the words and tell how the spelling patterns are similar.

Fluency

Remind children that good writing has good closure. Have each child read pages 12–14 aloud to end the text. Check to make sure each child is reading smoothly.

Comprehension

Review each child's Topic and Key Details graphic organizer, prompting children to explain the comprehension strategy and to talk through the graphic organizer.

Differentiated Instruction

- **Visual** learners can "see" the words by pointing to their favorite photographs of the town garden and talking about what they like in each.
- **Kinesthetic** learners can "feel" the words by acting out a visit to the town garden, including a picnic.
- **Auditory** learners can "hear" the words by following in their books while they listen to someone read it aloud.

Name_____

Word Web

Name _____

Topic and Key Details

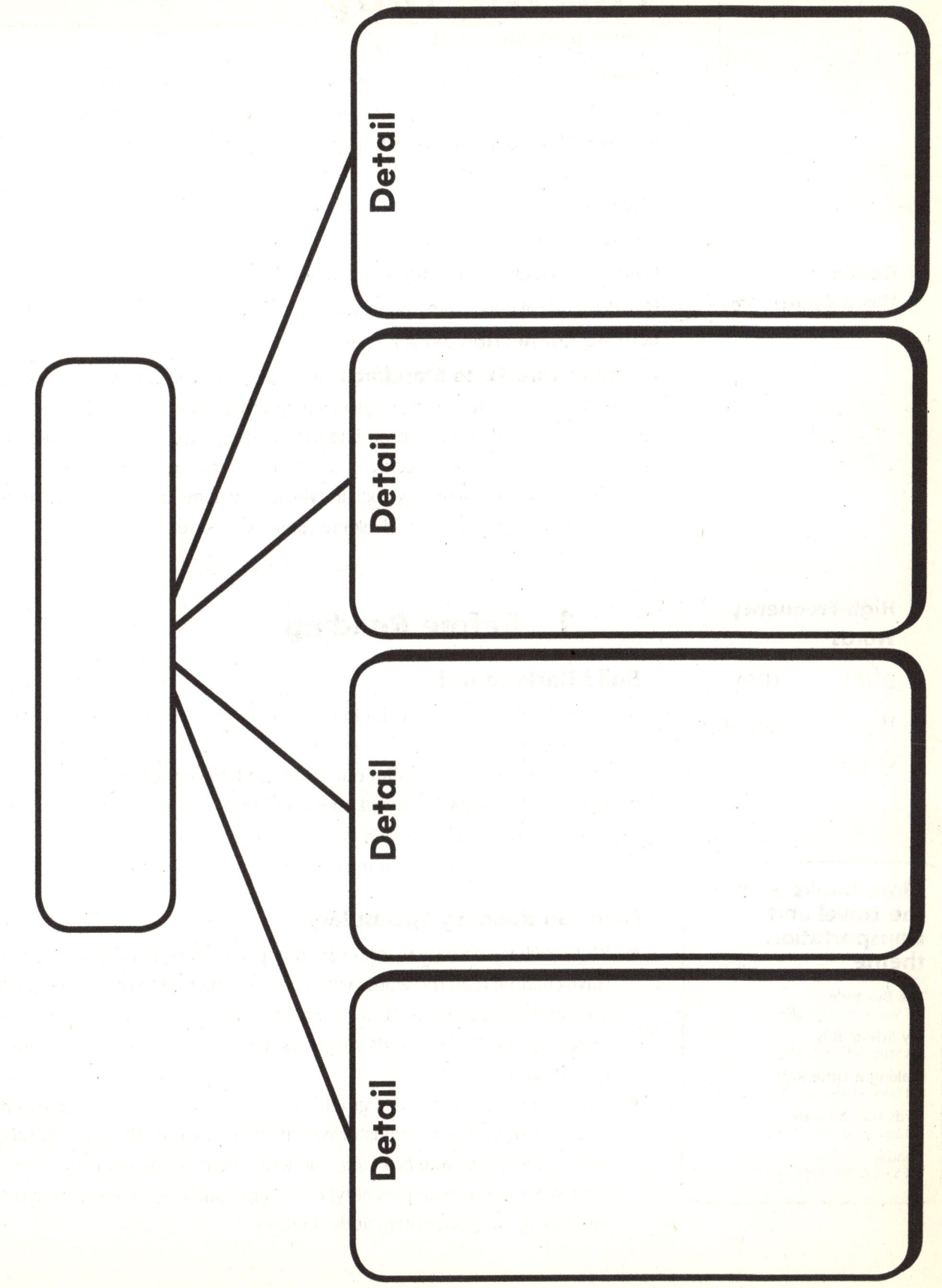

The Town Garden PM Stars Teacher's Guide—Yellow Level

43

The Big Ship
Written by Debbie Croft

Overview Moms and dads take a vacation on a big ship. The big ship has many rooms, swimming pools, and shops. What is a trip on this ship like?

Reading Vocabulary Words ship p. 2, captain p. 4, cabins p. 6, deck p. 9, pools p. 10, vacations p. 14

Phonics Skill Irregularly spelled words

Fluency Point Reading smoothly

Comprehension Strategy Describing connections within a text

Reading Strategy Using punctuation as you read

Writing Connection Book review

Common Core State Standards RI.1.3 Describe the connection between two individuals, events, ideas, or pieces of information in a text; RF.1.3g Recognize and read grade-appropriate irregularly spelled words; RF.1.4 Read grade-level text orally with accuracy, appropriate rate, and expression; W.1.2 Write informative/explanatory texts in which they name a topic, supply some facts about the topic, and provide some sense of closure.

Reading Word Count: 162

High-Frequency Words

after	they
it	outside
some	

More books within the travel and transportation theme

The Bus Ride
PM Stars Red Levels 5/6

My School Bus
PM Stars Red Levels 5/6

Making a Little Raft
PM Stars Yellow Levels 8/9

Birds that Migrate
PM Stars Blue Levels 11/12

Roads
PM Stars Green Levels 14/15

1 Before Reading

Build Background

- Read aloud the title with children. Point out the author's name. Say *This book is about a big ship.* Ask *What are some things you want to learn about the big ship?* Invite children to point out details and make predictions.
- Have children tell what they know about big ships that people travel on to take a vacation. *Where might the people be going?* Explain that some people go on big boats like this for a vacation.

Focus on Reading Vocabulary

- Write each vocabulary word on chart paper, reading it aloud as you write it. Have children read the words with you. Ask children to use the words to answer these questions: *Which words have two syllables? Which words mean more than one? Which words are places where you can go? Which words can have motion?*
- Model filling in a Word Map graphic organizer. Write the word *ship* in the diamond-shaped box. Brainstorm with children words that describe *ship*, such as *big, white,* and *beautiful,* and write them on the right. Then brainstorm some examples of types of ships, such as *sailing, navy, vacation,* and *fishing,* and write them at the bottom.

Focus on Phonics

Write the word *some* on the board. Say *Some is an irregular word because some of the letters do not make their usual sounds. We can't sound out the vowels in this word.* Point out that the word has a familiar pattern, but it doesn't help to read the word. Say *Some words you need to memorize how they are spelled and read.* Point to each letter in the word as children name the letters. Erase *some* and have children write it on paper. Repeat with *said* and *you*.

Focus on Fluency

Write on the board *There is a big ship on the water. I am going to be on that ship soon.* Model reading smoothly. Have children echo after you. Explain to students that good readers read smoothly. Say *When you read, the words should sound just like talking.* Point out that it does not sound choppy or stiff. Then have pairs practice reading the sentence until their reading is smooth.

Focus on Comprehension

Tell children that when they read nonfiction, they should notice how the information is connected, or similar. Help children deepen their understanding of how an author uses language to construct the message. Remind children that details provide information about a heading or subject. Say *As I read* The Big Ship, *I will think about how the details are similar.* Explain that this involves rereading to think about what the author is saying and how he or she says it.

2 Reading the Text

Have children read *The Big Ship*. As appropriate, monitor application of the comprehension strategy and support strategic reading using the prompts below.

Pages 2–3 Ask *What is the title of this section of the book?* Point out the three details given about the big ship. Say *I learned that the ship is slow, that it does not use sails, and that it uses big engines.* Ask *What connection can I make about these three details?* Point out that all the details describe how the big ship moves.

Pages 4–5 Say *I learned that the captain looks after the ship.* Model describing a connection between ideas in a text by pointing to the words *little room* in the second and third sentences. Say *The author mentions these words in two sentences. When I read these sentences, I make the connection that the little room is an important place for the captain.*

Pages 6–7 Ask *What is this section of the book telling you about the big ship? When you read smoothly, how should your voice sound?*

Pages 8–9 Say *These sentences continue to tell about ship's rooms. Both sentences say something about where moms and dads eat.* Ask *What is the author trying to tell me about eating on the ship?*

ESL/ELL

The digraph /sh/ may be difficult for some children to pronounce because it is not a sound in their home language. They may confuse the /sh/ sound with the /ch/ sound. Provide opportunities for them to listen to and practice saying words with the /sh/ sound.

Reading Strategy

Explain to children that they should use punctuation as they read. Review with children what a comma, period, exclamation point, and question mark signal. Point to the sentences on pages 2 and 3 of *The Big Ship*. Say *When I read I always pay attention to the punctuation. The punctuation tells me when to stop or pause. Using the punctuation helps me understand the message.* Model reading the page with and then without using the punctuation.

High-Frequency Words

For children who need additional practice, use the appropriate cards from the *PM High-Frequency Word Cards* boxed set. Pair children and have them take turns reading the high-frequency words.

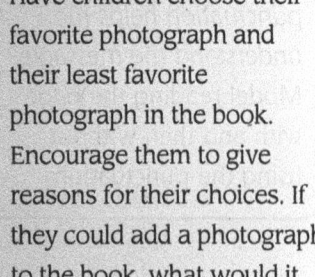

Visual Literacy

Have children choose their favorite photograph and their least favorite photograph in the book. Encourage them to give reasons for their choices. If they could add a photograph to the book, what would it be? Why would they choose this photograph to add?

Pages 10–11 Point out the title of this section. Ask *What will you read about in this section? Why do you think there are two swimming pools on the ship?* Point to the word *two* on page 10. Say *What makes this a difficult word to read?*

Pages 12–13 Say *Moms and dads go shopping on the ship, too. Think about what the book tells you about what people can do on a ship.* Ask *What can you say about people on a ship?*

Pages 14–15 Ask *Why do you think people like to take a vacation on the ship? Would you like to vacation on this ship? Why or why not?*

Independent Practice

Have children read the whole book independently at their own pace, using the Making Connections Within a Text graphic organizer for support as they read. Assist children in filling in two or more details from the text, and in describing a connection they make between the two details. Observe children as they read. Make note, mentally or in writing, how each child is or is not using the skills and strategies being focused on in this lesson.

3 Review

Reading Vocabulary

- Select a word, such as *vacation,* from this lesson's vocabulary list and model filling in the Word Map graphic organizer. Ask children to contribute their ideas for words that describe on the right and types of vacations at the bottom.
- Have children highlight, or add, the reading vocabulary words in their copies of *My PM Word Book*. Encourage children to use these words in their writing.

Phonics

Remind children that *some words do not make their usual sounds.* Say *You need to memorize how some words are spelled and pronounced.* Write *two* and *have* on the board and discuss how both words are irregular. Hold up individual word cards containing high-frequency words for this reading level. Have children raise their hands if a word is spelled irregularly. Have a volunteer explain why.

Fluency

Remind children to read smoothly, as if they are speaking. Choose a page in the book and have children practice reading it aloud until they can read the page smoothly.

Comprehension

Ask children to refer to their completed Making Connections Within a Text graphic organizers for *The Big Ship* as you lead a discussion about connections that can be made within the book. Prompt children to describe connections they made within *The Big Ship*.

Writing Connection

- Ask children to write a book report of *The Big Ship*. Tell children that a book report tells other people what the book is about. Have children write the title, author, and photographer at the top of their reports and to include three facts from the book. Explain that facts are true statements about a topic. Tell children that the author includes many details about the ship that are facts. Assist children in writing their sentences. Provide the following sentence stems:

    This book tells about_____ .
    I learned _____ .
    I also learned _____ .
    If you like _____, then you will enjoy this book.

- Remind children that it is important that they end their reports with a sense of closure. Point out the last sentence stem explaining that this sentence will provide a good way to end their report.

4 Assessment

Phonics

For each child provide the following list of words: *here, said, going, you, went, some,* and *with*. Have each child sort the words for regularly and irregularly spelled words. Ask children to read the sorted words aloud.

Fluency

Individually, have children read page 6 aloud. Check to make sure each child is using the punctuation correctly and reading the text smoothly.

Comprehension

Review each child's Making Connections Within a Text graphic organizer, prompting each child to explain the comprehension strategy and to talk through the graphic organizer.

Differentiated Instruction

- **Auditory** learners can "hear" the word by listening to someone read it while they read the book.
- **Visual** learners can "see" the words by pointing to favorite photographs in the beginning, middle, and end of the book.
- **Kinesthetic** learners can "feel" the story by acting out key events from the book.

Name_____

Word Map

Describe it!

Give examples!

48 The Big Ship PM Stars Teacher's Guide—Yellow Level

Name

Making Connections Within a Text

Title _____

Detail

Detail

Detail

→ Connection

The Big Ship PM Stars Teacher's Guide—Yellow Level

Telephones
Written by Elsie Nelley

Overview Telephones are machines that allow our voices to be heard far away. We use them every day. How do telephones help us?

Reading Vocabulary Words telephones p. 2, machines p. 2, numbers p. 3, letters p. 3, helpful p. 10

Vocabulary Skill Context Clues

Phonics Skill Long vowels

Fluency Point Reading phrases as mini-sentences

Comprehension Strategy Using text features

Reading Strategy Looking at the pictures

Writing Connection Report

Common Core State Standards RI.1.5 Know and use various text features to locate key facts or information in a text; RF.1.3c Know final -e and common vowel team conventions for representing long vowel sounds; RF.1.4b Read grade-level text orally with accuracy, appropriate rate, and expression; W.1.2 Write informative/explanatory texts in which they name a topic, supply some facts about the topic, and provide some sense of closure; L.1.4.b Use frequently occurring affixes as a clue to the meaning of a word.

Reading Word Count: 149

High-Frequency Words

with   us
some   she
her   help

More books within the communication and technology theme

Making a Toy Telephone
PM Stars Yellow Levels 8/9

Mailboxes
PM Stars Red Levels 5/6

A Guide Dog
PM Stars Blue Levels 11/12

1 Before Reading

Build Background

- Read aloud the title with children. Point out the author's name. Say *This book is about* telephones. *What is the boy doing? How does he seem to feel about using the telephone?* Invite children to point out details and make predictions.
- Have children tell what they know about telephones. Ask *Do you know what the buttons on a telephone are used for? How do you think using a telephone helps us every day? What do you think telephones will look like in the future?*

Focus on Reading Vocabulary

- Write each vocabulary word on chart paper, reading it aloud as you write it. Have children read the words. Ask children to answer these questions: *Which word names what you use to tell your age? Which word has three syllables? Which word names things that make our work easier? Which word names what your name is made of? Which word describes something?*
- Say *Sometimes a word part can be added to the end of a word to change the word's meaning.* Point out the ending *-ful* in the word *helpful*.
- Model filling in a Prefixes and Suffixes organizer. Write *helpful* in the first box. Say *In the word* helpful, *I see the familiar word* help *and the suffix* -ful. Write the root word and the suffix in the boxes of the equation. Say *A word part that is added to the end of the root word is a* suffix. *The suffix –ful means "full of."* Have children suggest a definition for the word. Repeat with *playful*.

Focus on Phonics

Write *note* on chart paper and say the word aloud. Then point to the vowel *o*. Say *When the first vowel in a one-syllable word is followed by a consonant and an* e, *the vowel is usually long and the final* e *is silent.* Underline the *o* and *e* and emphasize the /ō/ sound at the same time. Repeat with other CVCe words, such as *hope, made, bite,* and *cute*.

Focus on Fluency

Write the following sentence in one line on the board: *We ride in our car to visit our friends and our family.* Ask them to listen as you read it aloud. Say *The group of words* We ride in our car *is like a small sentence. You group words like this as you read, instead of reading them word by word.* Read the sentence again, grouping the words together. Have children read it chorally with you.

Focus on Comprehension

Explain that some nonfiction books include special features called a *glossary* and a *contents page*. These text features help readers better understand what they read. Direct children to the *Glossary* and *Contents* of *Telephones*. Explain that a glossary lists the important words in a book with a picture or an explanation of what the word means. A contents page lists the sections of a book and the page number where each begins.

2 Reading the Text

Guide the class, small groups, or individual students in reading the text, using the Text Features graphic organizer and the prompts below as appropriate.

Pages 2–3 Point to the words *numbers* and *letters*. Say *I know that words in bold print are important.* Ask *Where can I find more information about the important words in a book?* Turn to the glossary and use the photos to help explain the words.

Pages 4–5 Say *These sentences tell more about what telephones are.* Flip back one page to reveal the section heading. *They are in the section of the book called "What Are Telephones?"* Say *I know that all of the information in this section tells about what telephones are.*

Pages 6–7 Say *Look at the top of page 6.* Ask *What is the heading of this section of the book? Where else do you see this heading? How is the Contents page helpful?* Guide children to understand that the Contents page makes it easy to find information in a text. Ask *What will we read about in this section?*

Pages 8–9 Say *These sentences tell more about why people have telephones. Let's read the sentences about these little telephones on page 8 together. Remember to read groups of words together instead of reading word for word.*

ESL/ELL

After reading this book, review the vocabulary words and discuss what they mean. Then have children use the words to retell the information from the book. Correct children's pronunciation as necessary.

Reading Strategy

Remind children to use their skills and strategies when needed while they are reading. Say *One way to help yourself is to use the pictures to find out more information about a story or book. When you see a picture, you can ask How does this picture help me better understand what I am reading?* Model the skill using page 12. Begin to read, but stop before the word *doctor*. Say *I see a* doctor *in the picture.* Then, read the sentence to self-monitor, and say *Yes.* Doctor *makes sense.*

High-Frequency Words

For children who need additional practice, use the appropriate cards from the *PM High-Frequency Word Cards* boxed set. Pair children and have them practice writing the high-frequency words.

Visual Literacy

Have children look at the photograph on page 4. Ask *What does this photograph show us? What are the most important details in this photograph? How does this photograph help us better understand what we read on this page about how to make telephone calls? What caption or title would you write for this photograph?* Call on children to say their captions aloud.

Pages 10–11 Ask *What is the heading of this new section?* Point to the word *Helpful*. Say *This word includes suffix -ful. I know that this suffix means "full of." What will you read about in this section?*

Pages 12–13 Say *What is one way the book tells us that telephones are helpful?* Point to and pronounce the word *telephone*. Ask *Do you hear the long o sound in this word?* Cover up part of the word *telephone* to show the final syllable. Ask *What spelling pattern makes the long o sound in phone?*

Pages 14–15 Ask *How might the telephone help these people?* Discuss with children how the ending made them feel about the topic.

Independent Practice

To further support application of the comprehension skill, have children reread the book using the Text Feature graphic organizer for support. Work with children to write *Contents* or *Glossary* in the top box and to write how the text feature helps them in the bottom box. Observe children as they read. Make note, mentally or in writing, how each child is or is not using the skills and strategies being focused on in this lesson.

☆☆☆ 3 Review

Reading Vocabulary

- Review suffix *-ful*. Write *careful* on chart paper. Have a volunteer underline the suffix. Say *When I see suffix -ful, it helps me understand more about the word's meaning. This word means "full of care." A nurse is careful with sick patients.* Write the following words on chart paper: *cheerful, colorful, fearful, harmful.* Have children choose two words and complete a Prefixes and Suffixes graphic organizer.
- Have children highlight, or add, the reading vocabulary words in their copies of *My PM Word Book*. Encourage children to use these words in their writing.

Phonics

On chart paper, write *home* from page 8. Recall with children that in a one-syllable word followed by both a consonant and /e/, the vowel is long and the final /e/ is silent. Write the words *made, hope, try, cope, hi, be, like, gate,* and *wrote* on the board. Then write the headings CVCe and CV. Ask children to read the words aloud and sort the word under the appropriate heading.

Fluency

Remind children to think of groups of words, or phrases, as small sentences as they read. Have pairs practice by reading pages 8 and 10 aloud.

Comprehension

Ask children to refer to their completed Text Feature graphic organizers for *Telephones* as you lead a discussion about text features. Review specific information about a contents page, boldfaced words, and a glossary.

Writing Connection

- Tell children they will write a short report about a school activity, such as a game played at recess, a special event, or a class field trip. Provide topic suggestions for children, if needed.
- Tell children to identify three details and one fact about the topic to include in the report. Examples of facts would be the date of their school trip and how many students took part. Remind children that good writing includes a sense of closure. Ask *What is the feeling that you want the reader to have when the last words of your report have been read?* Brainstorm for ending sentences. Invite them to illustrate their report with a picture. Provide the following guide to assist children in their writing:
Name your topic.
Tell three things about the topic.
Draw a line under one fact.
Write a good ending.

4 Assessment

Phonics
Write the words *gate, life, hope, time, no,* and *made*. Have children circle the letters that make up the long vowel sounds in the words.

Fluency
Have children individually read aloud the last two sentences on page 8. Check to make sure each child reads the phrase in each sentence as a mini-sentence rather than reading it word by word.

Comprehension
Review each child's Text Feature organizer, prompting children to explain the comprehension strategy and to talk through the graphic organizer.

Differentiated Instruction

- **Kinesthetic** learners can "feel" the words by using a telephone to act out the information in the text.
- **Auditory** learners can "hear" the words by listening to someone read the text while they follow along in their books.
- **Visual** learners can "see" the text by drawing pictures that illustrate the answers to the headings in the Contents.

Name_____

Prefixes and Suffixes

[ ] + [ ] = [ ]

[ ] + [ ] = [ ]

This word means _____

This word means _____

Telephones PM Stars Teacher's Guide—Yellow Level

Name

Text Feature

Text feature from the book

What the text feature helps me understand

Telephones PM Stars Teacher's Guide—Yellow Level

Small Animals that Hide
Written by Elsie Nelley

Overview Many small animals have to hide to protect themselves. What are they hiding from? Where do they hide?

Reading Vocabulary Words hide p. 2, safe p. 3, fox p. 6, coat p. 6, insect p. 8, shell p. 10, pouch p. 14

Phonics Skill Consonant digraph *th*

Fluency Point Voice falling at end of declarative sentence

Comprehension Strategy Using text features

Reading Strategy Pointing to each word as you read

Writing Connection Book review

Common Core State Standards RI.1.5 Know and use various text features to locate key facts or information in a text; RF.1.3a Know the spelling-sound correspondences for common consonant digraphs; RF.1.4 Read grade-level text orally with accuracy, appropriate rate, and expression; W.1.1 Write opinion pieces in which they introduce the topic or name the book they are writing about, state an opinion, supply a reason for the opinion, and provide some sense of closure; L.1.5c Identify real-life connections between words and their use.

Reading Word Count: 170

High-Frequency Words

stay	white
of	like

More books within the protection and covering theme

Our Sunhats
PM Stars Red Levels 5/6

Making a Sunhat
PM Stars Red Levels 5/6

Looking for Frogs
PM Stars Red Levels 8/9

Big Animals That Hide
PM Stars Blue Levels 11/12

A Firefighter
PM Stars Green Levels 14/15

1 Before Reading

Build Background

- Read aloud the title with children. Point out the author's name. Say *This book is about small animals hiding.* Invite children to predict why small animals need to hide.
- Have children tell what they know about small animals. Explain that animals might hide from people or from other animals that want to eat them. Say *Where might a small animal hide?*

Focus on Reading Vocabulary

- Write each vocabulary word on chart paper, reading it aloud as you write it. Have children read the words with you. Ask children these questions: *Which word names an animal that has fur? Which word means that you are away from harm? Which word names an animal with six legs? Which word names something you can do? Which word names clothing? Which word names a type of covering? Which word names a place where a baby kangaroo can hide?*
- Explain to children that by making connections between words and ideas, we build vocabulary skills. Connections between vocabulary words make the process of building vocabulary skills faster and more efficient. Say *Sometimes a word reminds me of other things or makes me think of something else.* Write the word *coat* on chart paper. Have children repeat the word. Ask *What does the word coat remind you of?*

56 **PM Stars** Teacher's Guide

- Model filling in a Connections chart. Write *coat* in the circle. Brainstorm with children what this word reminds them of, what it makes them think of, things they've heard about, and things they've seen.

Focus on Phonics
Write the word *that* on chart paper. Explain that sometimes two consonants make a single sound. Say *When* t *and* h *are together, they make the sound* /th/. Point out the *t* and *h* and say /th/. Then say *that*. Write the words *the* and *they* on chart paper. Have children read each word and identify the digraph *th* in each.

Focus on Fluency
On the board, write a declarative sentence, such as *Every tiger has a different pattern in its fur.* Say *The period at the end of this sentence means I am telling you something. When you see a period at the end of a sentence, your voice should drop, or become lower.* Read the sentence aloud for children. Have the children repeat the sentence after you.

Focus on Comprehension
Explain that some nonfiction books include special features called a Contents page and headings. Tell children that using text features helps them understand information in the book. Direct children to look at the Contents page of *Small Animals that Hide.* Explain that a Contents page lists the sections of a book and the page number where each begins. Ask a volunteer to tell the page where one section begins. Turn to that section and point to the heading. Say *This is a heading.* The heading tells what you will learn in that section of the book.

2 Reading the Text

Have children read the book. As appropriate, monitor application of the comprehension strategy and support strategic reading using the prompts below.

Pages 2–3 Say *Name two details that you read about small animals.* Ask *What makes the hiding animals difficult to see?*

Pages 4–5 Say *Look at the top of page 4.* Ask *What is the heading of this section of the book? Where else do you see this heading? How is the Contents page helpful?* Guide children to understand that the Contents page makes it easy to find information in a text.

Pages 6–7 Ask *What is the heading for this section of the book? What do you think the author wants us to understand about color?* Have children point to a period and explain how to read the sentence.

Pages 8–9 Say *What did you learn about the shape of this small animal?* Point to the word *insect.* Say *How is an insect different from a fox? How are they the same?*

ESL/ELL
Different languages have different sounds. Some children may not be familiar with the /th/ sound. Demonstrate making the sound for children as you push your tongue between your teeth. Invite them to repeat after you. Have children take turns pronouncing such words as *thank, thin, thick,* and *thump.*

Reading Strategy
Explain to children that sometimes when they have difficulty reading, they should reread and point to each word to help make sense of the text. This will also help make sure that they don't miss any words. Say *When you point to each word as you read, you make sure you don't miss anything.*

Yellow **Levels 8/9**

High-Frequency Words

For children who need additional practice, use the appropriate cards from the *PM High-Frequency Word Cards* boxed set. Pair children and have them practice writing the high-frequency words.

Visual Literacy

Ask students to choose three to five images that, together, best summarize the text. Then pair students and have them take turns explaining their choices.

Pages 10–11 Point out that *shell* is boldfaced and that it is an important word for this topic. Have children find out more about the word in the glossary.

Pages 12–13 Ask *What is the heading for this section of* Small Animals that Hide? *How does the shape of a crab help it hide?*

Pages 14–15 Ask *Do you see a word that has letters* th? *Say the word* mother *and listen for the sound made by letters* th.. Point out the boldfaced word *pouch*. Ask *Why do you think this word is in bold type? Show me the text feature where I can find out more about the word.*

Independent Practice

To further support application of the comprehension skill, have children reread the book using the Text Feature graphic organizer for support. Work with children to write *Contents* or *Heading* in the top box and to write how the text feature helps them in the bottom box. Observe children as they read. Make note, mentally or in writing, how each child is or is not using the skills and strategies being focused on in this lesson.

3 Review

Reading Vocabulary

- Remind children that when they make connections between words and ideas, they are building vocabulary skills. Say *The more you think about words and how they are connected, the more you will understand about their meanings.* Write *safe*, *hide*, and *pouch* on the board. Have children choose one word and complete a Connections graphic organizer.
- Have children highlight or add the reading vocabulary words in their copies of *My PM Word Book*. Encourage children to use these words in their writing.

Phonics

Have children find and list words from *Small Animals that Hide* that begin with *th* in the text. (*that, the, they*)

Fluency

With a partner, have children take turns rereading pages 14 and 15, focusing on dropping their voices when they see a period at the end of a sentence.

Comprehension

Ask children to refer to their completed Text Feature graphic organizers for *Small Animals that Hide* as you lead a discussion about text features. Review specific information about a contents page, headings, boldfaced words, and a glossary.

Writing Connection

- Tell children they will write a book review about *Small Animals that Hide*. Explain that a book review is not a retelling of the book. A book review gives readers an idea of what a book is like and whether or not the reviewer enjoyed it. Provide the following guide to assist children in their writing:

  I read _____ .
  It is about _____ .
  The book is _____ because _____ .
  I think you will _____ .

- Explain that the book review will name the book, which is the topic of the review. It will include an opinion about the book and give a reason for the opinion. Discuss with children why they liked or disliked about *Small Animals that Hide* using specific examples. Remind children that the last part of their review leaves the reader with a feeling of "completeness."

4 Assessment

Phonics
Write *sing, bank, pick,* and *win* on the board. Have children write each word replacing the beginning letter with digraph *th* and read the new word.

Fluency
Individually, have children read pages 10 and 14 aloud. Check to make sure that each child drops his or her voice when they come to a period at the end of a sentence.

Comprehension
Review each child's Text Feature graphic organizer, prompting children to explain the comprehension strategy and to talk through the graphic organizer.

Differentiated Instruction

- **Tactile** learners can "feel" the words by placing a pretend green frog on a piece of green paper.
- **Auditory** learners can "hear" the words by working with partners and listening as one partner reads the text.
- **Visual** learners can "see" the words by looking at pictures of other small animals.

Name_____

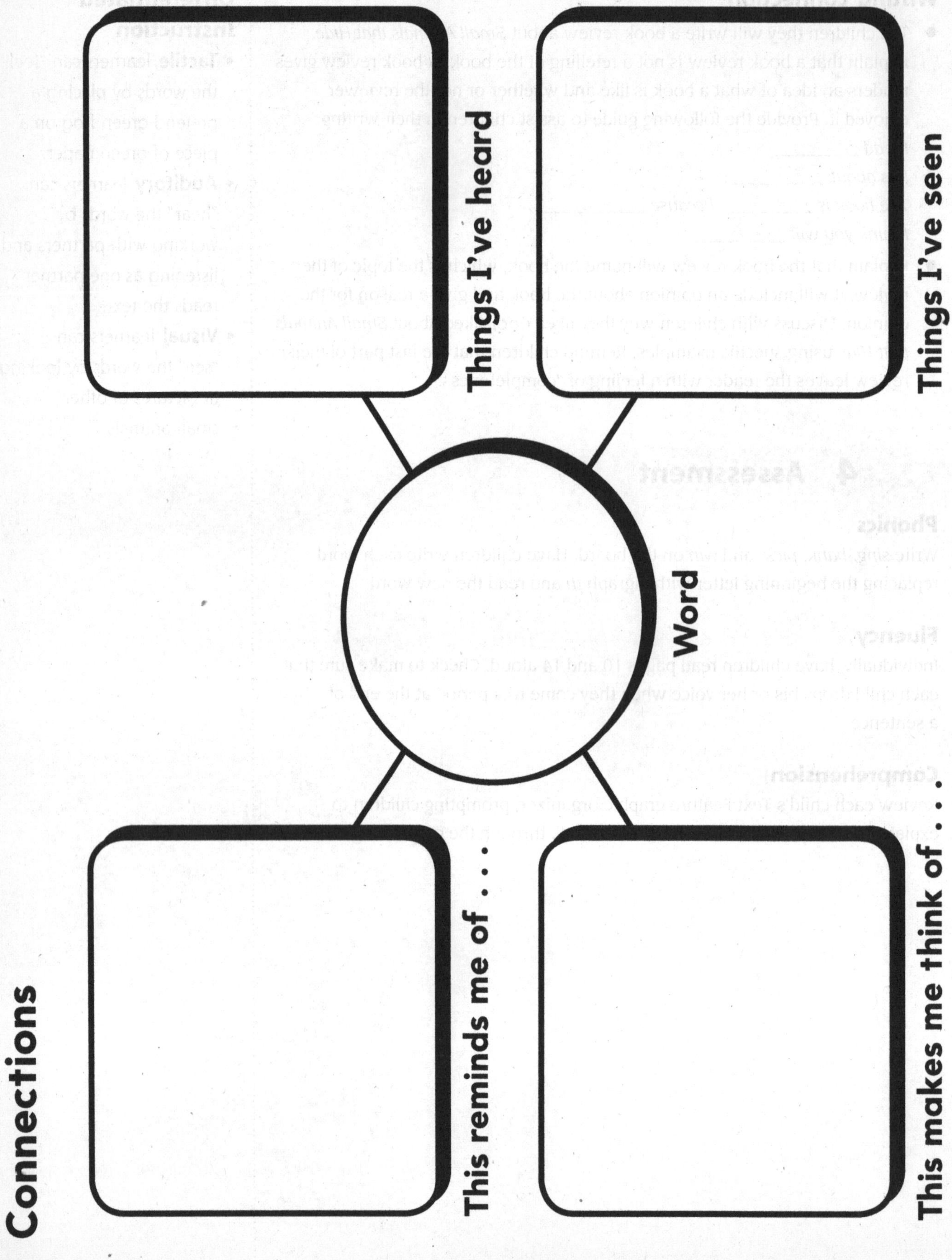

Connections

- Things I've heard
- Things I've seen
- Word
- This reminds me of . . . .
- This makes me think of . . . .

Small Animals that Hide PM Stars Teacher's Guide—Yellow Level

Name_____

Text Feature

Text feature from the book

What the text feature helps me understand

Small Animals that Hide PM Stars Teacher's Guide—Yellow Level

Our Vegetable Garden

Written by Sally Cowan   Photographs by Lyz Turner-Clark

Overview Children at a school plant a vegetable garden. They plant bean seeds and lettuce plants. They take care of the plants as they grow. What do you think the children will do with the beans and lettuce that they grow?

Reading Vocabulary Words vegetable p. 2, plant food p. 6, garden beds p. 6, lettuce p. 8, mulch p. 9

Vocabulary Skill Context clues

Phonics Skill Consonant digraph *ch*

Fluency Point Reading smoothly

Comprehension Strategy Identifying topic and key details

Reading Strategy Looking for another word you know

Writing Connection Explanation

Common Core State Standards RI.1.2 Identify the main topic and retell key details of a text; RF.1.3a Know the spelling-sound correspondences for commons consonant digraphs; RF.1.4b Read on-level text orally with accuracy, appropriate rate, and expression on successive readings; W.1.2 Write informative/explanatory texts in which they name a topic, supply some facts about the topic, and provide some sense of closure; L.1.4a Use sentence-level context as a clue to the meaning of word or phrase.

Reading Word Count: 116

High-Frequency Words

bigger   some
today   good

Additional leisure and work titles

The Town Garden
PM Stars Yellow Levels 8/9

Sandcastles
PM Stars Red Levels 5/6

The Face Painter
PM Stars Blue Levels 11/12

Clifton Market
PM Stars Green Levels 14/15

1 Before Reading

Build Background

- Introduce the book by reading aloud the title with children, discussing the photograph on the cover, and sharing the overview. Point out the author's name. Say *This is a photograph of children standing near a vegetable garden. Do the children look like they're having fun?* Invite children to point out details in the photograph to support their answers.

- Have children share what they know about vegetable gardens. Ask *Have you ever helped plant a garden? What did you do to take care of the plants?*

Focus on Reading Vocabulary

- Write the vocabulary words on chart paper and read them aloud. Ask children to use the words to answer these questions: *Which word describes beans, carrots, and peas? Which word names a place to plant a garden? Which word is something that you put on plants to make them grow? Which is a thing spread on the ground around plants? Which word names a vegetable found in salads?*

- Explain that the other words in a sentence are context clues. They can help readers figure out the meaning of an unknown word. They give readers an idea of the unknown word's meaning.

62 PM Stars Teacher's Guide

- Write *I like floral gardens because they have many flowers* on the board. Model filling in the Context Clues graphic organizer for the word *floral*. Write *gardens* and *many flowers* as words that help you understand the word, and *related to flowers* as the word's meaning.

Focus on Phonics
Write *chip* on chart paper and circle the digraph. Say *The letters* c *and* h *together make one sound, /*ch*/. In some words, like* chip, *the /*ch*/ sound is at the beginning of the word.* Write *Chelsea likes chocolate chip cookies.* Read the sentence aloud. Then have children circle the letters *ch* in the words, indicating whether the digraph is at the beginning, middle, or end of the word. Repeat with *Richard chopped each bunch of bananas.*

Focus on Fluency
Write the following sentence on the board: *I like lots of vegetables*. Have children follow along as you read the sentence aloud and echo read after you. Point out that you read the sentence smoothly, without stopping or repeating words. Be sure that children understand that reading smoothly does not mean reading fast.

Focus on Comprehension
Explain that nonfiction books have a main topic. Say *The topic is what the book is mostly about. The title of a book often tells the topic of the book.* Tell children that key details in a book tell important information about the main topic. Display the cover of a familiar nonfiction text. Have children identify the main topic. Flip through the sections of the book explaining that all the pages have key details about the main topic.

2 Reading the Text

Have children read *Our Vegetable Garden*. Monitor application of identifying topic and key details and support strategic reading using the prompts below.

Contents — Say *Remember, the title of a book tells the main topic of the book. The sections are about key details.*

Pages 2–3 — Talk with children about what the first step of making the garden might be. Ask *What key detail about making the vegetable garden is the first section about?*

Pages 4–5 — Have children identify the two details about the garden that this section is about. Ask *Where did the teacher go? What did he get?*

Pages 6–7 — Ask *What details about making the garden do you learn on these pages? Think about the meaning of* garden beds. *What words and phrases in the last sentence are clues to what* garden beds *are?*

ESL/ELL

The sound /ch/ may be difficult for some children to pronounce if it is not a sound in their home language. On index cards, write several words that do and do not have the /ch/ digraph. Invite pairs of children to work together to sort them into the two categories. Invite the pairs to explain their choices to other pairs.

Reading Strategy

Explain to children that they can use words they know on a page to figure out words they don't know. Point out the word *vegetables* on page 12. Say *I can use other words on the page to figure out the meaning of this word.* Read the sentence aloud skipping over *vegetables*. Say *The words tell me that the unknown word is something from the garden. The word I don't know begins with a* v, *and there are vegetables in the picture, so I think the word is* vegetables.

Yellow **Levels 8/9** 63

High-Frequency Words

For children who need additional practice, use the appropriate cards from the *PM High-Frequency Word Cards* boxed set. Have pairs of children take turns reading the words in random order.

Pages 8–9 Have children find the word that ends with the /ch/ sound spelled *ch*. Have them identify the sound that *c* and *h* make together and read the word aloud.

Pages 10–11 Ask *What is the main topic of this section? How is it a key detail of the main topic of the book, the vegetable garden?*

Pages 12–13 Say *Let's read the sentences on page 12 together. Remember to read smoothly.* Ask *When did you pause in your reading?* Ask *Are the vegetables a main topic or a key detail of the book?*

Pages 14–15 Say *What message does the author use to end the book? Is this a good ending? Why or why not?*

Independent Practice

To further support application of the comprehension skill, have children reread the book using the Topic and Key Details graphic organizer for support. Guide children in writing the main topic and key details from "The Garden Shop" section in the organizer. Observe children as they read. Make note of how each child is or is not using the skills and strategies being focused on in this lesson.

3 Review

Reading Vocabulary

- Select a reading vocabulary word or term, such as *plant food*, from this lesson's vocabulary list and model filling in the Context Clues graphic organizer. Have children contribute ideas to add to the organizer.
- Have children highlight, or add, the reading vocabulary words in their copies of *My PM Word Book*. Encourage them to use the words in their writing.

Phonics

On chart paper, write *lunch*. Recall with children the sound made by the consonant digraph *ch*. Practice with the sound with *mulch*, *chin*, and *bunch*.

Fluency

Remind children to read smoothly, not stopping in the middle of sentences or repeating words. Have pairs of children practice reading pages 2 and 4 to each other smoothly.

Comprehension

Ask children to refer to their completed Topic and Key Details graphic organizer for *Our Vegetable Garden* as you lead a discussion about the key details that were recorded.

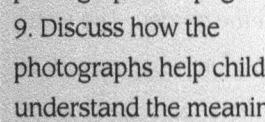

Visual Literacy

Have children study the photographs on pages 7 and 9. Discuss how the photographs help children understand the meaning of *garden beds* and *mulch*.

Writing Connection

- Say *An explanation is a type of writing in which a writer describes something* Tell children that they will write an explanation of a garden. Provide sentence frames to guide children's writing:

  A garden can have _____ .

  A garden needs _____ .

  A garden is _____ .

- Explain that writers supply facts in an explanation, such as what a garden is, what a garden can have growing, and what is needed to grow plants. Brainstorm with children two or three facts about what gardens need.

4 Assessment

Phonics
Have each child decode a word that includes the consonant digraph *ch*. Use the words *pinch, check, such,* and *chose*.

Fluency
Have children individually read page 10. Check that each child reads smoothly.

Comprehension
Review each child's Topic and Key Details graphic organizer, prompting each child to explain the comprehension strategy and to talk through the graphic organizer.

Differentiated Instruction

- **Auditory** learners can "hear" the story by carefully listening for the words *vegetable* or *vegetables* as the story is read aloud. Tell them to clap each time they hear either word.
- **Kinesthetic** learners can "feel" the words by pantomiming the action of the children as they prepare their garden.
- **Visual** learners can "see" the words by painting a picture of the different plants growing in the vegetable garden.

Name_____

Context Clues

words I don't know

words that help me understand

word's meaning

Name _____

Topic and Key Details

- Detail
- Detail
- Detail
- Detail

Our Vegetable Garden PM Stars Teacher's Guide—Yellow Level 9

Meg's Family

Written by Annette Smith   Photographs by Lindsay Edwards

Overview Meg lives with her mom and dad. They own a book store. After school, Meg stays with Gran and Grandad, who live on the same street. What kinds of things do you think Meg does with her family?

Reading Vocabulary Words DVDs p. 4, cameras p. 6, photos p. 6, computer p. 8, yard p. 10

Vocabulary Skill Context clues

Phonics Skill Spelling pattern *CVCe*

Fluency Point Pausing at commas

Comprehension Strategy Identifying topic and key details

Reading Strategy Skipping the word, reading on, and then rereading

Writing Connection Book review

Common Core State Standards RI.1.2 Identify the main topic and retell key details of a text; RF.1.3b Decode regularly spelled one-syllable words; RF.1.4b Read on-level text orally with accuracy, appropriate rate, and expression on successive readings; W.1.1 Write opinion pieces in which they introduce the topic or name the book they are writing about, state an opinion, supply a reason for the opinion, and provide some sense of closure; L.1.4a Use sentence-level context as a clue to the meaning of a word.

Reading Word Count: 147

High-Frequency Words

white	after
her	they
with	

More books within the families theme

Kris's Family
PM Stars Yellow Levels 8/9
Anna's Family
PM Stars Yellow Levels 8/9
Cam's Family
PM Stars Yellow Levels 8/9

 **1 Before Reading**

Build Background

- Read aloud the title with children. Point out the author's name, talk about the cover photograph, and share the overview. Say *Here is Meg with people in her family. Who else could be in Meg's family?* Invite children to point out details and make predictions about Meg's family.
- Have children tell what they know about families. Invite children to share information about their own families. Ask *Who is in your family? What kinds of things do you do with the people in your family?*

Focus on Reading Vocabulary

- Write each vocabulary word on chart paper and read it aloud. Ask children to use the words to answer these questions: *Which word names something used only to take pictures and videos? Which word is a kind of image? Which word names a thing with a screen that people use for work and play? Which word names a place at a house where people play and garden? Which is a thing that has images people can look at on a computer?*
- Explain that to figure out an unknown word, a reader can look at other words in a sentence for clues. Read aloud the second sentence on page 6. Point out that the word *photos* is a clue to the meaning of the word *camera*.

68 PM Stars Teacher's Guide

- Model filling out the Context Clues organizer. Write the following sentence on the board: *My ferret is a good pet.* Tell students that you will use context clues to figure out the word *ferret*. In the middle box, write *A pet is an animal.* Think aloud as you figure out the word's meaning, and then write that information in the bottom box (*A ferret is an animal*).

Focus on Phonics
Write *I like birthday cake best of all* on chart paper and read the sentence aloud. Circle the *i* in *like*. Say *like*, emphasizing the long vowel *i* sound. Say *The word like has the spelling pattern consonant-vowel-consonant-silent e (CVCe). When words have this spelling pattern, the e at the end is not pronounced and the vowel sound is long.* Underline the word *cake*. Have children identify the CVCe spelling pattern in *cake* and read the word. Create a word sort to practice this skill.

Focus on Fluency
Write on the board *I like cats, dogs, and rabbits*. Point out the commas. Explain that commas are signals that tell readers to pause, or stop for a short time. Read the sentence to model fluent reading. Have children suggest alternate items in a series. Change the sentence accordingly, and read it chorally with children.

Focus on Comprehension
- Display a familiar nonfiction book. Say *Nonfiction books are often about one main topic. What is this book mostly about? That's its main topic. When you know the main topic, you can understand the information the author gives.*
- Say *The title of a book often tells the topic of the book. Let's read the title of this book.* Display the front and back cover of *Meg's Family* and read the title. Say *I think this book is about a girl named Meg and her family.*
- Add that key details give more information about the main topic. Explain that inside the book, there are details about the main topic, Meg's family.

2 Reading the Text

Have children read *Meg's Family*. As appropriate, monitor application of the comprehension strategy and support strategic reading using the prompts below.

Contents — Remind children that the Contents is a list of the sections in a book. Ask *What detail is the second section about? The fourth?*

Pages 2–3 — Say *Meg and her family are the main topic of this book. What information is a key detail about Meg's family?*

Pages 4–5 — Ask *Who are these pages about? How are the details related to the main topic?* Point out the commas in the second sentence. Ask *What should you do when you get to a comma while reading?* Choral read the sentences with children.

ESL/ELL
Tell children that the word *DVD* is an abbreviation, a shortened form of a word. Write the following sentence on the board: *We got a new DVD, and I was very excited to watch the movie.* Use context clues to figure out what DVDs are. Explain to children that even if they don't know what the letters stand for, they can use context clues to figure out the word's meanings.

Reading Strategy
Explain to children that when they come to a word they don't know or can't sound out, they can skip the word and read on to the end of the sentence. Say *The rest of the sentence may give clues to figure out what the word is or what it means. When you think you know the word, reread the sentence and see if the word makes sense in it.*

Yellow Levels 8/9

High-Frequency Words

For children who need additional practice, use the appropriate cards from the *PM High-Frequency Word Cards* boxed set. Have children practice reading and spelling the words.

Visual Literacy

Have children identify the photograph that offers the most details about Meg's family. Ask them to tell what they learned about Meg or a family member from the photograph they chose.

Pages 6–7 Ask *How are the details about Meg's mom related to the main topic?* Point to the word *photos* in the second sentence. Ask *What words in the sentence help you understand the meaning of photos?*

Pages 8–9 Review with children the members of Meg's family they have read about so far. Ask *What details have you learned about Meg's dad? How are they related to the main topic?* Point to the word *home*. Say *There is an e at the end of the word. What o sound should the word have? How do we say this word?*

Pages 10–11 Ask *What details about the main topic is this section about?* Have children find the commas and choral read the page pausing at the commas.

Pages 12–13 Have children restate the main topic of the book in their own words. Ask *How do Gran and Grandad help take care of Meg?*

Pages 14–15 Ask *What message does the author give to the reader about the main topic? How does the ending leave you feeling?*

Independent Practice

To further support application of the comprehension skill, have children reread the book using the Topic and Key Details graphic organizer for support. Have children fill in the organizer with key details about Mom, Dad, Gran, and Grandad. Observe children as they read. Make note of how each child is or is not using the skills and strategies being focused on in this lesson.

3 Review

Reading Vocabulary

- Select a word, such as *cameras*, from this lesson's vocabulary list and model filling in the Context Clues graphic organizer. Ask children to contribute their ideas for words that help them understand and for the word's meaning.
- Have children highlight, or add, the reading vocabulary words in their copies of *My PM Word Book*. Encourage them to use the words in their writing.

Phonics

Recall with children how to identify and read syllables with the CVCe spelling pattern. On chart paper, write *game*. Circle the *e* and ask how it affects the vowel *a* sound. Have children read the word. Repeat with *like*, *home*, *make*, and *cake*.

Fluency

Remind children to pause, or stop for a short while, when they come to commas in the text. Have pairs of children practice by reading page 10.

Comprehension

Ask children to look at their completed Topic and Key Details graphic organizer for *Meg's Family* as you lead a discussion about the key details recorded.

Writing Connection

- Say *A book review is a piece of writing that tells an opinion of a book. Let's write a book review of* Meg's Family. Have children prepare by listing words or phrases about why they did or did not like the book.
- Guide children to begin their review by naming the book's title and author. Have them continue with sentences that tell whether they liked the book. Provide sentence frames to guide children's writing:

  I read _____.
  I liked the book.
  I liked it because _____.
  This book is _____.

4 Assessment

Phonics

Have each child decode a word with the CVCe spelling pattern and explain the associated spelling rule. Use the words *flake*, *dome*, and *slime*.

Fluency

Individually, have children read page 4 aloud. Check to make sure that each child pauses at the commas.

Comprehension

Review each child's Topic and Key Details graphic organizer, prompting the child to explain the comprehension strategy and to talk about the graphic organizer.

Differentiated Instruction

- **Auditory** learners can "hear" the words by closing their eyes and listening to the book being read.
- **Kinesthetic** learners can "feel" the words by acting out the text.
- **Visual** learners can "see" the words by drawing a picture of Meg's whole family for the book.

Name_____

Context Clues

words I don't know

⬇

words that help me understand

⬇

word's meaning

Name_____

Topic and Key Details

- Detail
- Detail
- Detail
- Detail

Meg's Family PM Stars Teacher's Guide—Yellow Level

Making a Toy Telephone
Written by Elsie Nelley   Photographs by Lindsay Edwards

Overview In this book, you will read about how to make a toy telephone using some simple materials. We can make one with just two plastic cups, a pencil, a ball of string, and scissors. Will the telephone work?

Reading Vocabulary Words telephone p. 2, plastic p. 3, materials p. 3, pencil p. 3, scissors p. 3, talk p. 14, friend p. 14

Phonics Skill Irregularly spelled words

Fluency Point Accurately pronouncing difficult words

Comprehension Strategy Distinguishing information from pictures and text

Reading Strategy Looking at the end of the word

Writing Connection Book recommendation

Common Core State Standards RI.1.6 Distinguish between information provided by pictures or other illustrations and information provided by the words in a text; RF.1.3g Recognize and read grade-appropriate irregularly spelled words; RF.1.4c Use context to confirm or self-correct word recognition and understanding, rereading as necessary; W.1.1 Write opinion pieces in which they introduce the topic or name the book they are writing about, state an opinion, supply a reason for the opinion, and provide some sense of closure.

Reading Word Count: 85

High-Frequency Words

with	stay
some	like

Additional travel and transportation titles

The Bus Ride
PM Stars Nonfiction Red Levels 5/6

The Big Ship
PM Stars Nonfiction Yellow Levels 7/8

Making a Little Raft
PM Stars Nonfiction Yellow Levels 7/8

Birds that Migrate
PM Stars Nonfiction Blue Levels 11/12

 **1 Before Reading**

Build Background

- Read aloud the title with children. Point out the author's name, talk about the cover photograph, and share the overview with children. Say *The children have made a toy telephone. How do you think they made it?* Invite children to point out details and make predictions.
- Have children tell what they know about telephones. Ask *For what do people use a telephone? How many people usually use one telephone at the same time?*

Focus on Reading Vocabulary

- Write the vocabulary words on chart paper. Read each word aloud. Ask children to use the words to answer these questions: *The book explains how to make something. Which word names the thing you will learn to make? Which word is another word for the things we need to make the telephone? Which word is something we use to cut with? Which word tells us what we can do when we're done making the phone? Who might we do it with?*
- Model filling in a Word Map about the word *telephone*. In the top left shape, write the word *telephone*. In one of the right-hand circles, write something to describe what you can do with a telephone, such as *talk to a friend*. In one of the boxes below, write a type of phone, such as *cell phone*.

Focus on Phonics

Say *Some words are difficult to read. They do not follow a regular spelling pattern, so they are not easy to sound out.* Write the following words on index cards and read them aloud: *friend, come, could,* and *again.* Say *We can't sound out the vowels in these word. We need to memorize how it they are spelled and read.* On the board, write the words leaving blanks in the place of some letters, for example fr_end. Have children fill in the missing letter(s). Reveal the word card for children to check the spelling.

Focus on Fluency

Explain that one way for readers to confirm the pronunciation of an unfamiliar word or correct their mispronunciation is to look in the sentence for clues to the word's meaning. Write the following sentences on the chart paper: *I cut the green paper with scissors. I gave a nice gift to my friend. I looked for the word in the glossary.* Explain that the phrase "cut the green paper" helps you know what *scissors* are and how to read the word. Point to *scissors* as you lead children in echo reading the sentences.

Focus on Comprehension

Say *In a book, both the words and the pictures provide information. The words tell details and the pictures show details. When you think about information you learned from a book, recall whether the information is from text or from a picture. The cover of a book often shows the title of the book and an image. Let's look at the cover of* Making a Toy Telephone. *What information does the title give and the picture show?*

 2 Reading the Text

Have children read *Making a Toy Telephone*. As appropriate, monitor application of the comprehension strategy and support strategic reading using the prompts below.

Pages 2–3 Point out the heading *Goal*. Say *Remember that words and photographs provide information. Which gives you information to figure out the meaning of* goal, *the sentence or the photograph?*

Pages 4–5 Ask *What detail about using the pencil do the words tell that the photographs do not show?*

Pages 6–7 Say *I read that I need to cut some string, but not how much string to cut. Where is that detail provided? If you only looked at the photographs, would you know what to do with the string?*

Pages 8–9 Ask *From which do you learn how the string goes into each cup, the text or the photographs?*

Pages 10–11 Talk with children about which they did first: read the text or look at the photographs. Ask *How do you know how to make the string stay in each cup?*

ESL/ELL

Show children the pictures on page 2, but not the text. Remind children that they can get important information from the pictures and the pictures can help them figure out the words. Have children tell you what the label would be for each picture, then show them what the book says.

Reading Strategy

Explain to children that they can use their skills and strategies to figure out unknown words while they are reading. Say *Look at the end of an unknown word for clues to what the word is. For example, see if the word ends with -s or -e, or -ing. A word that ends in -s might be a plural noun. A word that ends in -e might have a long vowel sound in the last syllable.*

High-Frequency Words

For children who need additional practice, use the appropriate cards from the *PM High-Frequency Word Cards* boxed set. Have pairs of children place the word cards facedown and take turns choosing and reading one at random.

Visual Literacy

Ask students to choose the four to six most important pictures in the text. Have them look for photos that could provide enough information with the text for someone to make the toy telephone. Then pair students and have them take turns explaining their choices to their partners.

Pages 12–13 Explain that sometimes the words in a book could give more information. Ask *What more information could be written to help you understand how the telephone should look now?*

Pages 14–15 Point to the word *friend*. Say *Look at the beginning and end of each word. Count its syllables. Look for spelling patterns that you know. Can you pronounce this word?* Repeat with *telephone*

Page 16 Point to the word *glossary*. Ask *Can you pronounce this word? If you only read the text or only looked at the photos, would you know what this word is?*

Independent Practice

To further support application of the comprehension strategy, have children reread the book using the Distinguish Information from Pictures and Text graphic organizer for support. Guide children in writing key details from the book and identifying where the detail was observed. Observe children as they read. Make note of how each child is or is not using the skill being focused on in this lesson.

3 Review

Reading Vocabulary

- Select a word, such as *plastic*, from this lesson's vocabulary list and model filling in the Word Map graphic organizer. Ask children to contribute their ideas for words that describe it and an example of it.
- Have children highlight, or add, the reading vocabulary words in their copies of *My PM Word Book*. Encourage children to use these words in their writing.

Phonics

On the chalkboard or chart paper, write *was, are,* and *blue*. Remind children that sometimes words don't follow regular spelling patterns. Read the words aloud as children echo. Create individual cards for the letters of each word. Have children build the words.

Fluency

Have children read page 3, 6, or 14 aloud. Say, *Remember, after you read a difficult word, look in the rest of the sentence for clues to what the word means and confirm its pronunciation.*

Comprehension

Ask children to refer to their completed Distinguish Information from Pictures and Text graphic organizers for *Making a Toy Telephone* as you lead a discussion about the questions and answers children recorded.

Writing Connection

- Say *People write book recommendations to suggest that something is good or worth doing. A book recommendation includes the name of the book, why the writer likes the book, and a suggestion that others read the book.* Tell children that they will write a recommendation to read *Making a Toy Telephone*. Provide the following sentence frames to guide children's writing:

  I read _____.
  I liked it because _____.
  You should _____.

- Discuss the importance of an ending that provides closure. Point out the last sentence and encourage children to provide an ending with a suggestion for readers to follow, such as *You should get this book from your school library today!*

4 Assessment

Phonics
Using flash cards, check children's pronunciation of the following irregularly spelled words: *come, could, again, was, are,* and *blue*. Add additional cards with difficult words from other books that children are reading.

Fluency
Have each child read page 6 or 14 aloud. Listen to determine whether the child is accurately pronouncing difficult words when encountering them, or self-correcting after making an error.

Comprehension
Review each child's Distinguish Information from Pictures and Text graphic organizer, prompting the child to explain the comprehension strategy and talk through his or her graphic organizer.

Differentiated Instruction

- **Kinesthetic** learners can "feel" the words by making their own toy telephone.
- **Auditory** learners can "hear" the words by listening to someone read the narrative while they read along in the text.
- **Visual** learners can "see" the words by drawing pictures of the sequence of making a toy telephone.

Name_____

Describe it!

Word Map

Give examples!

78 Making a Toy Telephone PM Stars Teacher's Guide—Yellow Level

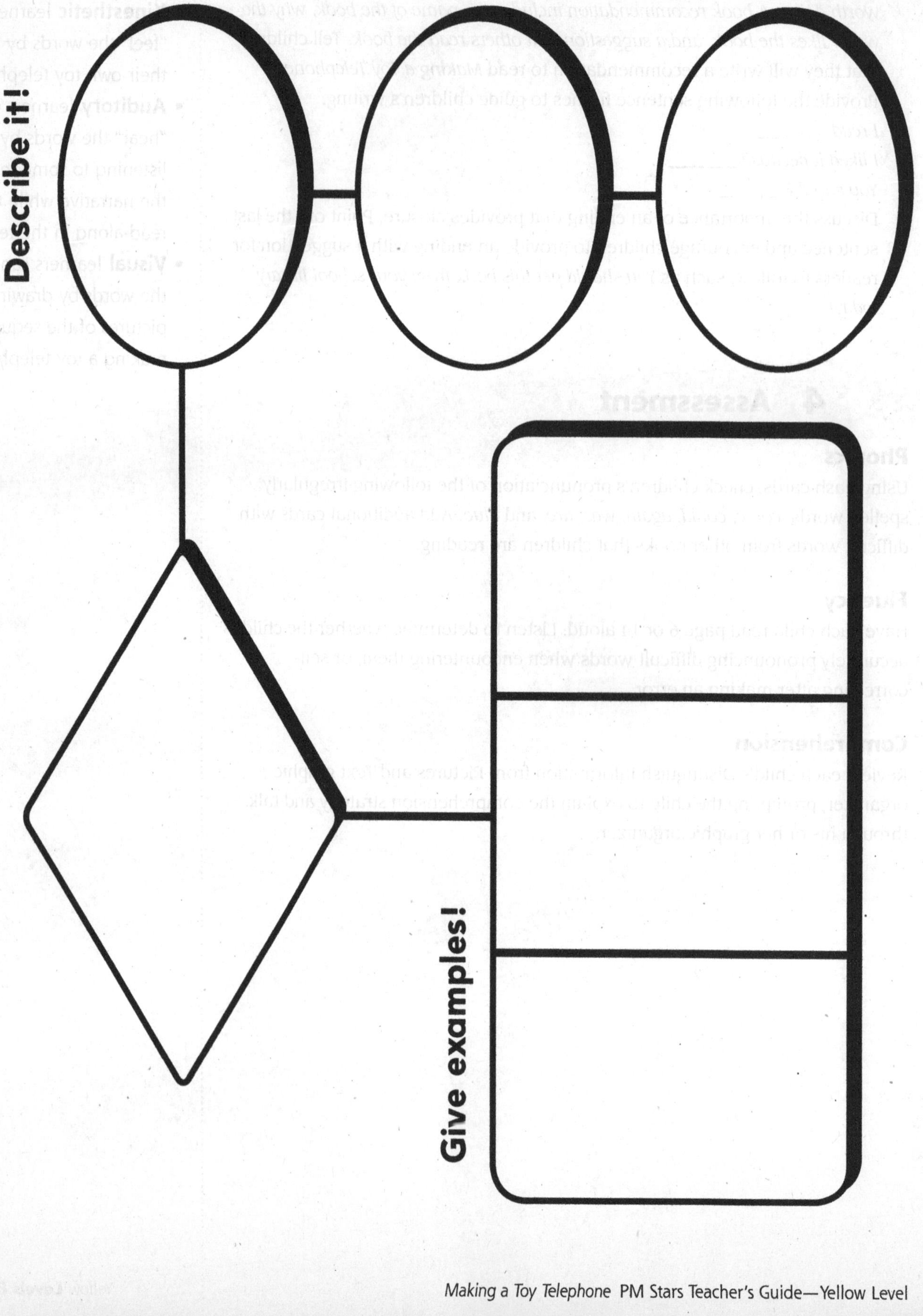

© Houghton Mifflin Harcourt. All rights reserved.

Name_____

Distinguish Information from Pictures and Text

Key Details	page	from the picture (✓)	from the book (✓)

Making a Little Raft

Written by Debbie Croft   Photographs by Lindsay Edwards

Overview You can make a little raft using some simple materials. You will need some sticks, string, play dough, cardboard, and water. Do you think the little raft will float?

Reading Vocabulary Words raft p. 2, goal p. 2, materials p. 2, dough p. 3, scissors p. 3, sail p. 10, mast p. 13

Phonics Skill Spelling pattern *CVC*

Fluency Point Reading phrases as mini-sentences

Comprehension Strategy Distinguishing information from pictures and text

Reading Strategy Thinking about what comes next and if it makes sense

Writing Connection Recommendation

Common Core State Standards RI.1.6 Distinguish between information provided by pictures or other illustrations and information provided by the words in a text; RF.1.3b Decode regularly spelled one-syllable words; RF.1.4b Read on-level text orally with accuracy, appropriate rate, and expression on successive readings; W.1.1 Write opinion pieces in which they introduce the topic or name the book they are writing about, state an opinion, supply a reason for the opinion, and provide some sense of closure.

Reading Word Count: 108

High-Frequency Words

yellow   with
like   out
some   get

Additional travel and transport titles

The Bus Ride
PM Stars Red Levels 5/6
The Big Ship
PM Stars Yellow Levels 7/8
Birds that Migrate
PM Stars Blue Levels 11/12
Bike Safety
PM Stars Green Levels 14/15

1 Before Reading

Build Background

- Read aloud the title with children. Point out the author's name, talk about the cover photograph, and share the overview. Say *The boy is smiling. Why do you think that is?* Invite children to point out details and make predictions.
- Have children tell what they know about rafts. Ask *What does a raft need to do? What can a raft be made of?*

Focus on Reading Vocabulary

- Write the vocabulary words on chart paper. Read each word aloud. Ask children to use the words to answer these questions: *Which word is the subject of the book? Which word names all the items you need to make the raft? Which word names something we use to cut with? Which words are parts of the raft?* Say *If someone follows these steps and makes a little raft, they have met a goal.* This means that they have done what they set out to do.
- Model filling in a Word Sorter Chart graphic organizer. At the top, write the word *raft*. In the next left box, write *parts of the raft*. In the right box, write *materials*. Fill in the chart with vocabulary words, such as *mast* and *scissors*.

Focus on Phonics

Say *We know many spelling patterns. One of them is the spelling pattern consonant-vowel-consonant (CVC). When words have this spelling pattern, the vowel sound is usually short.* Write *The big red bike had a bow* on chart paper and read the sentence aloud. Circle the *i* in *big*. Point out the CVC spelling pattern. Say *big*, emphasizing the short vowel *i* sound. Have children identify the CVC spelling pattern and short vowel sound in *red* and *bow*.

Focus on Fluency

Write the following sentence in one line on the board: *It's my favorite book even though it's very long*. Ask children to listen as you read it aloud. Say *The group of words* It's my favorite book *is like a small sentence. You group words like this as you read, instead of reading them word by word*. Read the sentence again, grouping the words into phrases: *It's my favorite book / even though / it's very long*. Have children read it chorally with you.

Focus on Comprehension

Explain *Readers can get information from the words and from the images in a text. Both the words and the images have details. Readers can use the details in words and images to understand what they read*. Display a page with text and a photograph, diagram, or illustration from a familiar nonfiction book. Have children describe the image and what information they learn from it. Note children's ideas on chart paper, then read the text on the page. Ask *What information is in the text? What information did we find in the image?*

2 Reading the Text

Have children read *Making a Little Raft*. As appropriate, monitor application of the comprehension strategy and support strategic reading using the prompts below.

Pages 2–3 Have children think about the materials listed and shown. Ask *Which items from the materials list are parts of the raft? From where did you get that information, the words or the photographs?*

Pages 4–5 Remind children to read phrases as mini sentences. Say *Look at the heading and at each sentence. Which words can you group like a small sentence?* Ask *Where is the information about where to put the big sticks and the little sticks?*

Pages 6–7 Cover the photographs on the pages and read the text. Ask *Do you know exactly what to do with the string?* Display the photographs with the text. Ask *Now do you know how to use the string now? Which word has the CVC spelling pattern? What is the vowel sound in the word? Read the word* cut.

ESL/ELL

After reading this book, use the photographs and text to review the vocabulary words. Say each word, then ask children to point to both the word and its picture.

Reading Strategy

When children are reading, remind them to think about what might come next. Say *When I have difficulty, I think about what would come next. After I read, I ask myself if it makes sense*. Remind children to always reread to self monitor after using a reading strategy.

High-Frequency Words

For children who need additional practice, use the appropriate cards from the *PM High-Frequency Word Cards* boxed set. Have children review the words on the cards and then select two or three words to use in a short sentence.

Pages 8–9 Ask *What detail in the photographs show you where to put the ball of play dough?*

Pages 10–11 Ask *Where do you learn where to put the yellow stars, in the words or in the photographs?*

Pages 12–13 Explain that sometimes photographs could show more details. Ask *How do the photographs help you understand what to do? What else could the photograph of Mom cutting the holes show?*

Pages 14–15 Ask *Where do you see that the little raft can go on water? Are you surprised that the little raft floats? Why or why not?*

Independent Practice

To further support application of the comprehension skill, have children reread the book using the Distinguish Information from Pictures and Text graphic organizer for support. Have children note details and then identify where the detail was noticed. Observe children as they read. Make note of how each child is or is not using the skills and strategies being focused on in this lesson.

3 Review

Reading Vocabulary

- Select a word, such as *mast*, from this lesson's vocabulary list and model filling in the Word Sorter Chart graphic organizer. Ask children to contribute their ideas for words that describe it and an example of it.
- Have children highlight or add the reading vocabulary words in their copies of *My PM Word Book*. Encourage children to use these words in their writing.

Phonics

Recall with children what the CVC spelling pattern is and how it affects the vowel sound in a word. On chart paper, write *can*. Circle the *a* and ask children what sound it makes. Have children read the word. Repeat with *tub*, *raft*, and *stick*.

Fluency

Have children read pages 12 or 13 aloud. Remind them to group words into phrases like small sentences as they read the long sentences.

Comprehension

Ask children to refer to their completed Distinguish Information from Pictures and Text graphic organizer for *Making a Little Raft* as you lead a discussion about the photographs in the book.

Visual Literacy

Ask students to choose four to six important pictures that might provide enough information for someone to make the little raft. Then pair students and have partners take turns explaining their choices.

Writing Connection

- Say *A book recommendation is written to suggest that a book is good.* Explain that a book recommendation has several parts. Say *First, the writer names the book. Next, the writer tells why he or she likes the book. Then the writers ends with a suggestion for readers.* Provide the following sentence frames to guide children's writing:

  I read _____.

  I liked it because _____.

  Now you should _____.

- Brainstorm reasons why children like the book, *Making a Little Raft.* Remind children of the importance of a good ending to their writing. Encourage children to end their writing with a suggestion for readers, such as *Now you should read this book to learn to make a little raft.*

 **4 Assessment**

Phonics
Have each child decode one or two words with the CVC spelling pattern. Use the words *six, sticks, cut, get, red,* and *tub.*

Fluency
Have children individually read pages 14 and 15 aloud. Listen to determine whether each child is grouping words into phrases.

Comprehension
Review each child's Distinguish Information from Pictures and Text graphic organizer, prompting the child to explain the comprehension strategy and talk through the graphic organizer.

Differentiated Instruction

- **Kinesthetic** learners can "feel" the words by using the same materials to make their own little raft and seeing it float.
- **Tactile** learners can "feel" the words by handling the various materials required to build the raft.
- **Visual** learners can "see" the words by drawing pictures of the sequence of the raft instructions.

Yellow **Levels 8/9** 83

Name_____

Word Sorter

84

Making a Little Raft PM Stars Teacher's Guide—Yellow Level

Name_____

Distinguish Information from Pictures and Text

Key Details	page	from the picture (✓)	from the book (✓)

Making a Little Raft PM Stars Teacher's Guide—Yellow Level

Looking for Frogs

Written by Elsie Nelley   Photographs by Lyz Turner-Clark

Overview A girl and her dad go to a pond to look for frogs. They see a brown lizard and some green bugs. Will they be able to find a frog?

Reading Vocabulary Words frogs p. 2, lizard p. 4, grass p. 4, plant p. 6, swimming p. 8, jumped p. 10

Vocabulary Skill Root words

Phonics Skill Inflected ending -ed

Fluency Point Voice falling at end of declarative sentence

Comprehension Strategy Using text features

Reading Strategy Checking for a pattern

Writing Connection Explanation

Common Core State Standards RI.1.5 Know and use various text features to locate key facts or information in a text; RF.1.3f Read words with inflectional endings; RF.1.4b Read grade-level text orally with accuracy, appropriate rate, and expression; W.1.2 Write informative/explanatory texts in which they name a topic, supply some facts about the topic, and provide some sense of closure; L.1.4c Identify frequently occurring root words and their inflectional forms.

Reading Word Count: 136

High-Frequency Words

one	some
day	green
brown	all

Additional protection and covering titles

Our Sun Hats
PM Stars Red Levels 5/6

Making a Sun Hat
PM Stars Red Levels 5/6

Small Animals that Hide
PM Stars Yellow Levels 8/9

A Lion's Hideaway
PM Stars Blue Levels 11/12

Big Animals that Hide
PM Stars Blue Levels 11/12

Fire on the Farm
PM Stars Green Levels 14/15

A Firefighter
PM Stars Green Levels 14/15

 **1 Before Reading**

Build Background

- Introduce the book by reading aloud the title with children. Point out the author's name. Say *The girl is pointing to something.* Ask *What do you think she is looking at?* Invite children to point out details and make predictions.
- Have children tell what they know about frogs. Ask *Where would be some good places to look for frogs? Do you think they are hard to find? Why or why not?*

Focus on Reading Vocabulary

- Write the Reading Vocabulary words on blank cards. Hold up each word, read it aloud, and help children provide definitions. Point out that all the words are either animals, places where animals live, or actions. Display one of each, such as *frogs, swimming,* and *plant,* and have children make sentences.
- Say *A root word is a word that other parts are added to in order to make new words. If you don't know a long word, try looking for a root word in it that you do know.* Write *jumped* on chart paper and work with children to circle the root word, *jump.* List other forms of the word, such as *jumping, jumps,* and *jumper.*
- Introduce the Root Words graphic organizer. Write the word *swimming* in the right-hand box. Ask children to identify the root word, *swim,* and write it in the "root word" box. Brainstorm with children other forms of *swim* and write them in the right-hand box.

Focus on Phonics

Tell children that looking for endings they know will help them read longer words. Write *lasted* on chart paper. Say *One word ending we know is -ed.* Ask children to identify the ending, and then circle it. Point out the part that is left is a word they know. Guide children to understand that this ending can have different sounds. Model with *backed* and *played*, pointing out the /t/ and /d/ pronunciations of *-ed*.

Focus on Fluency

Write the following sentence on the board: *I like to dance in the rain.* Read the sentence and ask children to tell what your voice did at the end. Point to the period at the end of the sentence and say *When you see a period, let your voice fall as you read the end of the sentence.* Model reading the sentence again. Then have children read the sentence, letting their voices fall at the end.

Focus on Comprehension

Remind children that nonfiction books have text features that help readers understand and find information in the text. Display a boldface glossary word in a familiar nonfiction book. Say *When a word in a nonfiction book is bold, it is a glossary word. You can find the meaning of the word in the* glossary. Turn to the Glossary page and point out the word. Explain that a glossary includes difficult or important words from the text and is usually found in the back of the book.

2 Reading the Text

Have children read *Looking for Frogs*. As appropriate, monitor application of the comprehension strategy and support strategic reading using the prompts below.

Pages 2–3   Ask *Where are the girl and her dad going? What are they going to do there?* Point out the boldface word *pond*. Ask *Why is this word in bold text? Where can we look to find out what it means?*

Pages 4–5   Ask *What is the girl looking for? What did she see instead?* Point to the vocabulary word *lizard* and have children recall its meaning. Ask *Which picture helps you understand the word?*

Pages 6–7   Ask *Has the girl found what she is looking for yet?* Have children identify the glossary word. Ask *How can we find the meaning of this word?* If needed, prompt children to turn to the Glossary at the back of the book. Discuss how it shows the meaning of *bugs*.

Pages 8–9   Ask *Where does the girl look next? What does she see?* Point out the period at the end of each sentence. Ask *How do we read a sentence that ends with a period?* Model reading sentence 1. Then have children read sentences 2 and 3.

ESL/ELL

Some English-language learners may have difficulty producing the /d/ and /t/ made by the inflected ending *-ed* since the sounds do not exist in their first languages. Provide a list of one-syllable words ending in /d/ and /t/, such as *sand* and *gate*, for extra practice producing the *-ed* sounds.

Reading Strategy

Explain to children that noticing a pattern, such a repeated phrases, can help them read. Say *Some books have a pattern in the text that happens again and again. Look at page 4. The girl tells about seeing a lizard in sentences 1 and 2. What does she say in sentence 3? Now look at page 6. What does the girl tell about first? What sentence is the same as on page 4?* Discuss how the pattern continues, with small changes, on page 8.

High-Frequency Words

For children who need additional practice, use the appropriate cards from the *PM High-Frequency Word Cards* boxed set. Have children write a sentence for each word.

Visual Literacy

Have children identify a favorite photo and a least favorite photo in the book. Prompt them to discuss specific aspects of each photo that helped them make their choices.

Pages 10–11 Point to *jumped* and have children identify the root word. Ask *What does* jumped *mean in the sentence? Does it make sense that the frog jumped? Why?*

Pages 12–13 Say *The girl and the frog look at each other. Then the frog goes back into the water. How do you think the girl feels? How do you think the frog feels?* Have children explain their answers.

Pages 14–15 Ask *What was the girl looking for at the beginning of the book? Which animal does she like seeing the best? Why do you think she likes frogs?* Point to the word *liked* on page 14. Remind children to look for endings and have them read the word.

Page 16 Remind children that the Glossary tells the meaning of difficult words in the text. Ask *What are bugs? What is a pond?* Discuss how looking up the bold glossary words helped children understand the text.

Independent Practice

To further support application of the comprehension skill, have children reread the book using the Text Feature graphic organizer for support. Assist children in filling in the organizer to tell how the glossary words and Glossary page helped them understand the text. Observe children as they read. Make note of how each child is or is not using the skills and strategies being focused on in this lesson.

3 Review

Reading Vocabulary

- Provide children with a copy of the Root Words organizer and write *picked* on the board. Ask children to identify the root word, and write *pick* in the "root word" box. Write *picked* in the "other forms" box. Ask children to add other forms of the root word, such as *picking*, *picks*, and *picker* to the organizer.
- Have children highlight, or add, the reading vocabulary words in their copies of *My PM Word Book*. Encourage children to use these words in their writing.

Phonics

Remind children to look for endings they know to help them read longer words. On the board, write *asked, landed,* and *hiked*. Ask children what ending they see in all of these words. Recall with children the sounds of the *-ed* ending. Call on volunteers to read each word aloud and have the class echo them.

Fluency

Remind children that their voice should fall when they read a sentence that ends in a period. Have groups of children take turns reading the sentences on page 8 aloud.

Comprehension

Ask children to refer to their completed Text Feature organizer for *Looking for Frogs* as you lead a discussion about the features that were recorded.

Writing Connection

- Tell children they will be writing an explanation. Say *An explanation is writing that explains how something works or why it is how it is.* Provide children with examples of explanation topics, such as how a pen works or why cats have whiskers. Have children think of something they would like to explain. Have children write their explanation using the following sentence stems:

    I will explain _____.
    This happens because _____.
    Also _____.
    Another fact is _____.
    That is [why/how] _____.

- Say *An explanation must tell the topic, or what you are explaining. It must also have facts, or true information, that tell about the topic.* Guide children to brainstorm facts related to their explanation topics.

4 Assessment

Phonics

Listen to each child read the following words with the inflected *-ed* ending: *wished, nested, liked, tried.*

Fluency

Individually, have children read a page of the text aloud. Listen to determine if each child is allowing his or her voice to fall at the end of each sentence.

Comprehension

Review each child's Text Feature organizer, prompting the child to explain the comprehension strategy and to talk through the graphic organizer.

Differentiated Instruction

- **Tactile** learners can "feel" the words by touching objects from the book, such as a leaf, water, or living creatures, such as a lizard or frog.
- **Auditory** learners can "hear" the words by listening to someone read the narrative while they read along in the text.
- **Visual** learners can "see" the words by drawing pictures of their favorite creature and least favorite creature, including details such as color and habitat.

Name_____

Root Words

other forms

↑

root word

Name_____

Text Feature

Text feature from the book

What the text feature helps me understand

Kris's Family

Written by Elsie Nelley   Photographs by Lindsay Edwards

Overview Kris and his family like animals. Kris's mom takes care of animals. The family has many different animals. What kinds of animals do they have?

Reading Vocabulary Words photo p. 2, sister p. 2, farm p. 4, animals p. 6, dog p. 8, cat p. 10, bird p. 12, pony p. 14

Vocabulary Skill Word sorts

Phonics Skill Inflected ending -s

Fluency Point Adjusting pace

Comprehension Strategy Using text features

Reading Strategy Getting your mouth ready for the first letter's sound

Writing Connection Book recommendation

Common Core State Standards RI.1.5 Know and use various text features to locate key facts or information in a text; RF.1.3f Read words with inflectional endings; RF.1.4b Read grade-level text orally with accuracy, appropriate rate, and expression; W.1.1 Write opinion pieces in which they introduce the topic or name the book they are writing about, state an opinion, supply a reason for the opinion, and provide some sense of closure; L.1.5a Sort words into categories to gain a sense of the concepts the categories represent; L.1.5b Define words by category and by one or more key attributes.

Reading Word Count: 158

High-Frequency Words

like   her
outside   yellow
inside

More books within the family series

Playing with Jip
PM Stars Red Levels 5/6

Cam's Family
PM Stars Yellow Levels 7/8

Meg's Family
PM Stars Yellow Levels 7/8

Anna's Family
PM Stars Yellow Levels 8/9

Horses
PM Stars Blue Levels 11/12

Taking Care of a Bird
PM Stars Green Levels 14/15

1 Before Reading

Build Background

- Introduce the book by reading aloud the title with children. Point out the author's name. Say *This must be Kris's family. Where do you think they might live? What do you think they like to do together?*
- Have children tell what they know about getting a pet. Say *What pet would you like to have? What would you need if you had that pet? Who would take care of your pet?*

Focus on Reading Vocabulary

- Write the Reading Vocabulary words on the board. Read each word aloud and ask children to tell what they know about it. Support children's understanding with pictures as needed. Provide sets of two words and have children use them in sentences.
- Remind children that a category is a group of things that are alike. Say *Think about how words are alike to sort them into categories.* Have children tell the vocabulary word that could be a category for a number of other vocabulary words. Then have children generate other categories that vocabulary words could fit into, like pets, four legs, living things, things you find in the country, etc. Ask children to tell a key fact about each word, such as *A bird is an animal with wings.*

92 **PM Stars** Teacher's Guide

- Model filling in a Word Sorter graphic organizer. Write the categories *Smaller* and *Larger* in the two second-tier boxes. Have children sort the vocabulary words into the boxes below the two categories based on whether things are smaller or larger than themselves.

Focus on Phonics

Tell children that looking for endings they know will help them read words. Write *smiles* on chart paper. Say *One word ending we know is -s.* Ask children to identify the ending, and then circle it. Point out the part that is left is a word they know. Guide children to read the word by thinking of the separate parts, the main word and the ending, pointing out the /z/ pronunciation of the *-s* ending. Repeat with *makes, grows, runs, and writes* pointing out the /s/ and /z/ pronunciations of the *-s* ending.

Focus on Fluency

Say *Your reading pace is how fast or slow you read. Good readers slow down or speed up depending on what they are reading.* Choose a slightly above-level text and model reading more slowly when you come to longer, more difficult sentences and speeding up again to read shorter, easier sentences. Write and say aloud *I go horseback riding at the farm every weekend.* Have children read the sentence, making sure to slow down a little to say all the words smoothly.

Focus on Comprehension

Remind children that nonfiction books have text features that help readers understand the text and find information. Show the table of contents from familiar nonfiction book. Say *The* table of contents *shows what each chapter in the text is about and where we can find it.* Read a chapter title and have children tell what page it starts on. Turn to that page in the text, point to the matching chapter heading, and say *A chapter heading* tells what information is in the chapter. Discuss with children what information they will find in this chapter.

2 Reading the Text

Have children read *Kris's Family.* As appropriate, monitor application of the comprehension strategy and support strategic reading using the prompts below.

Page 1   Point out the Contents section and have children read the four chapter titles. Ask *On what page can we read about Kris's mom and dad?* Ask children to recall the meaning of the word *animal.* Ask *Where should we look for details about Kris's pets?*

Pages 2–3   Point to the "My Family" heading at the top of the page. Ask *What will this chapter be about?* Prompt children to read the text to check their answer. Ask *What is Kris doing in the picture?*

ESL/ELL

Some English-language learners may have difficulty pronouncing the -s ending correctly because the sound doesn't exist or *s* makes a different sound in their home language. Point out that the -s ending makes the /z/ sound most of the time. It only makes the /s/ sound after the final sounds /p/, /t/, /k/, and /f/. Provide children with extra practice reading the -s ending in words with different final sounds.

Reading Strategy

Explain to children that a helpful reading strategy is noticing the first letter of a word and getting your mouth ready to make the sound. Say *If you come to a word you don't know, stop and look at the first letter of the word.* Model reading the sentence up to *family* and saying /f/. Say *The photo the boy is holding is of his family.* Reread the sentence to self-monitor, then say *Starting the word helped me read the sentence.*

High-Frequency Words

For children who need additional practice, use the appropriate cards from the *PM High-Frequency Word Cards* boxed set. Pair children and have them take turns reading the high-frequency words.

Visual Literacy

Have children examine the photograph on page 13. Ask *What does this photo show? Which details help you understand what is happening?* Then have children write a brief caption that describes the photograph for the reader.

Pages 4–5 Ask *Is this still the "My Family" chapter? How do you know? What details do you see on this page about Kris's family?* Point to the vocabulary word *farm*. Ask *Do Kris and Mia live in the city or in the country? How do you know? Where do they play on the farm?*

Pages 6–7 Point to the chapter heading. Ask *What will this chapter be about?* Point out the long last sentence on page 6. Have children read sentences 3 and 4 aloud, slowing down to read the difficult sentence smoothly. Ask *What does a vet do?*

Pages 8–9 Have children identify the chapter heading and predict what the chapter is about. Then say *I see a word on page 8 with the -s ending.* Have children identify and read *likes*. Ask *Who is Jip? What does Jip like to do?*

Pages 10–11 Ask *How is the family's cat different from their dog?* Say *You read two -s ending words on this page. How did you say them?*

Pages 12–13 Have children recall the chapter heading on page 8. Ask *What other pet does Kris's family have? What have all the details in this chapter been about so far?*

Pages 14–15 Ask *How is the pony different from the family's pets?* Point out the last sentence. Ask *How is this a good ending to this chapter?*

Independent Practice

To further support application of the comprehension skill, have children reread the book using the Text Feature graphic organizer for support. Assist children in filling in the organizer to tell how the table of contents and chapter headings helped them find information and understand the text. Observe children as they read. Make note of how each child is or is not using the skills and strategies being focused on in this lesson.

3 Review

Reading Vocabulary

- Provide children with a copy of the Word Sorter organizer. Write *Four legs* and *Two legs* in the second-tier boxes. Have children tell which vocabulary words fit in each category, reminding them to not just look at animal words. Model writing the words in appropriate boxes.
- Have children highlight, or add, the reading vocabulary words in their copies of *My PM Word Book*. Encourage children to use these words in their writing.

Phonics

Remind children to look for endings they know to help them read words. Have children find words with the -s ending on pages 6, 10, and 12. Then have them read the sentences that contain these words.

Fluency Review

Remind children that when they read aloud, they should slow down a bit to be able to read more difficult words and sentences smoothly. Have pairs of children practice reading page 10 aloud, adjusting their pace to read smoothly.

Comprehension Review

Ask children to refer to their completed Text Feature organizer for *Kris's Family* as you lead a discussion about the features that were recorded.

Writing Connection

- Tell children they will be writing a book recommendation for *Kris's Family*. Say *A recommendation tells why someone should read this book.* Explain that not only does a recommendation promote a book, it also gives a reason why the book is recommended. Discuss with children reasons why they liked the book. Have children write their recommendation using the sentence stems:
  You should read the book _____.
  It is good because _____.
  I also liked _____.
  It will teach you _____.

- Point to the sentences as you discuss the structure of the recommendation. Explain to children that the topic is mentioned first, and the reasons are next. Say *Remember to tell your topic, or what you are writing about, and your recommendation, or what you want people to do.*

4 Assessment

Phonics

Have each child find a word with the inflected ending -s in the text and read the sentence containing the word.

Fluency

Individually, have children read pages 2 and 6 aloud. Check to make sure that they read at a pace that allows them to maintain fluency.

Comprehension

Review each child's Text Feature organizer, prompting the child to explain the comprehension strategy and to talk through the graphic organizer.

Differentiated Instruction

- **Visual** learners can "see" the words by making a "Pet and Vet" collage with pictures from magazines.
- **Auditory** learners can "hear" the words by reading the book aloud with children in a small group.
- **Kinesthetic** learners can "feel" the words by using puppets or stuffed animals to play vet.

Name_____

Word Sorter

96

Kris's Family PM Stars Teacher's Guide—Yellow Level

Name_____

Text Feature

Text feature from the book

What the text feature helps me understand

Cam's Family

Written by Sally Cowan   Photographs by Lindsay Edwards

Overview Cam lives in a house with his mom and his sister, Lee. Mom likes to paint pictures. Sometimes Cam and Lee stay with their dad. Dad plays the violin. What do Cam and Lee like to do with their mom and their dad?

Reading Vocabulary Words upstairs p. 4, paints p. 4, art p. 5, teacher p. 5, school p. 5, park p. 8

Vocabulary Skill Connections

Phonics Skill Inflected ending -ing

Fluency Point Taking a breath at appropriate times

Comprehension Strategy Asking and answering questions

Reading Strategy Looking at the words from left to right

Writing Connection Personal narrative

Common Core State Standards RI.1.1 Ask and answer questions about key details in a text; RI.1.4 Ask and answer questions to help determine or clarify the meaning of words and phrases in a text; RF.1.3f Read words with inflectional endings; RF.1.4b Read grade-level text orally with accuracy, appropriate rate, and expression; W.1.3 Write narratives in which they recount two or more appropriately sequenced events, include some details regarding what happened, use temporal words to signal event order, and provide some sense of closure; L.1.5c Identify real-life connections between words and their use.

Reading Word Count: 158

High-Frequency Words

she	stay
with	good
like	

More books in the family series

Dinosaur Day at School
PM Stars Red Levels 5/6

Meg's Family
PM Stars Yellow Levels 7/8

Anna's Family
PM Stars Yellow Levels 8/9

Kris's Family
PM Stars Yellow Levels 8/9

Murals
PM Stars Blue Levels 11/12

A Dinosaur Mural
PM Stars Green Levels 14/15

1 Before Reading

Build Background

- Introduce the book by reading the title with children. Point out the author's name. Point to the boy in the center and ask *Who do you think this is*? Point to the two smaller photos. Ask *Who do you think these people are?*
- Offer examples of several kinds of family units. Invite children to share information about their own families. Ask *Who is in your family? What kinds of things do you do with people in your family?*

Focus on Reading Vocabulary

- Write Reading Vocabulary words across the top of chart paper to form columns. Read each word aloud and ask children to share what they know about it. Add to their knowledge as needed and write details in the columns. Have children work in pairs to write a sentence for each word.
- Say *A good way to learn and remember what a word means is by thinking about how it connects to your life*. Model making a real-life connection to *upstairs* based on your personal experience. Then have children volunteer some real-life connections they can make to vocabulary words.

- Model filling in the Connections graphic organizer, writing *park* in the Word box. Prompt children to share things *park* reminds them of, makes them think of, and things they have seen and heard. Write responses in the appropriate surrounding boxes.

Focus on Phonics
Remind children that looking for endings they know will help them read longer words. Write *singing* on chart paper. Say *One word ending we know is* -ing. Ask children to identify the ending. Circle *ing* and point out the part that is left is a word they know. Guide children to read the word by thinking of the separate parts, the main word and the ending. Repeat with *willing* and *flying*.

Focus on Fluency
Write with line breaks at the slashes *I am a teacher, / and I work / at a school. I teach first grade. / I get to school every day / at 8 o'clock in the morning.* Circle the commas and underline the periods. Say *Fluent readers take breaths in places that make sense. You can take short breaths at commas and longer breaths at periods. If you must take a breath in a long sentence without a comma, take a quick breath between groups of words that go together.* Erase the slashes in sentences 1 and 2. Model breathing at commas and periods having children echo your reading.

Focus on Comprehension
Say *Remember as you read to think about what you are reading. If you think of a question, look for the answer as you read. Asking and answering questions helps you understand what you read.* Display the cover and ask children to tell what questions they have about what they will be reading. Write questions on the board and encourage children to look for answers as they read the book.

2 Reading the Text

Have children read *Cam's Family*. As appropriate, monitor application of the comprehension strategy and support strategic reading using the prompts below.

Pages 2–3 Point out the word *I*. Ask *Who is "I," in this book?* Have children read the page aloud, making sure to breathe appropriately at commas and periods. Guide them to breathe between phrases if they must take a breath in the middle of the last sentence.

Pages 4–5 Have children generate questions about Cam, his sister, his mom, or where they live. Prompt children to look at the text and pictures to find answers. Point to *upstairs*. Ask *What does this word tell you about Cam's house?*

Pages 6–7 Point to the heading "Going to School." Ask *What questions can we ask about this chapter? Where might we find the answers?* Point to the word *Going*. Ask *How should we read this* -ing *word?*

ESL/ELL

To help English language learners generate details for their writing, have them fill in a Word Web about a time they did an activity with a family member. Allow them to draw pictures or write single words to describe the activity. Then work with them to put their details into English words and phrases that they can use in their personal narratives.

Reading Strategy

Remind children to read words from left to right. Draw children's attention to the first sentence on page 4. Slide your finger from left to right as you say the words. Ask *Which word did I read first? Which word did I read next?* Say *Yes, we always read from left to right.* Then have children read the next two sentences, always reading from left to right.

High-Frequency Words

For children who need additional practice, use the appropriate cards from the *PM High-Frequency Word Cards* boxed set. Group children. Have them each write a sentence for each high-frequency word and then compare sentences.

Visual Literacy

Have children work together to find a photograph that includes Cam. Ask *What are some words that tell about Cam in this picture? What is Cam doing? What is he wearing? Does he look happy?*

Pages 8–9 Guide children to ask questions about what Cam and Lee do at Dad's house. Encourage them to keep reading to find the answers. Point to the vocabulary word *park*. Ask *What do you think Cam, Lee, and Dad do at the park?*

Pages 10–11 Point out the boldfaced words. Say *Remember, we can find the meanings of these words in the Glossary at the back of the book.*

Pages 12–13 Ask *How do the details on this page help answer some of your questions? Do you think Cam likes listening to Dad and Lee play? How can you tell?*

Pages 14–15 Have children identify the *-ing* word in the chapter head and read the heading. Ask *What do Cam and Lee do at home with Mom? What do they do at Dad's house?* Review with children questions they asked as they read and where they found the answers.

Independent Practice

To further support application of the comprehension skill, have children reread the book using the Questions and Answers Chart graphic organizer for support. Assist children in filling in the chart with questions and finding answers as appropriate from the text and pictures. Observe children as they read. Make note of how each child is or is not using the skills and strategies being focused on in this lesson.

 3 Review

Reading Vocabulary

- Give children copies of the Connections organizer. Write *art* in the center space. Work with children to identify their real-life connections to the word. Model writing the connections in the appropriate boxes.
- Have children highlight, or add, the reading vocabulary words in their copies of *My PM Word Book*. Encourage them to use the words in their writing.

Phonics

Write the word *making* on chart paper. Remind children to look for endings they know to help them read longer words. Guide children to find the *–ing* ending in the word on the board and read it. Then have children practice with the words: *painting, pulling, running*.

Fluency

Remind children to only take breaths at appropriate times, such as at commas, periods, and between groups of words. Have pairs of children practice by reading pages 12, 14, and 15 aloud.

Comprehension

Ask children to refer to their completed Questions and Answers Chart for *Cam's Family* as you lead a discussion about the questions and answers that were recorded.

Writing Connection

- Tell children they will write a personal narrative. Recall that a personal narrative is a true story from the life of the writer. Ask children to think about an activity they did with a family member. Have children write their narratives by completing the sentence stems:

  I _____ with _____.
  First we _____.
  Then _____.
  Finally we _____.
  We had a _____ day.

- Say *Good writers give details about what happened in their narratives.* Point out that the middle three sentence stems helped children add details about what they did with their family member. Say *Giving details helps readers understand exactly what happened.*

4 Assessment

Phonics

Write the following words on the board: *going, talking, make, baking, walked, eating, hopped, playing.* Have children identify and read the words that have the *-ing* ending.

Fluency

Have individual children read page 8 aloud. Check to make sure each child takes a breath at appropriate times.

Comprehension

Review each child's Questions and Answers Chart, prompting the child to explain the comprehension strategy and to talk through the graphic organizer.

Differentiated Instruction

- **Auditory** learners can "hear" the words by closing their eyes and listening to the book being read to them.
- **Kinesthetic** learners can "feel" the words by using figures of people to act out the text.
- **Visual** learners can "see" the words by drawing a picture of Cam with some family members.

Name_____

Connections

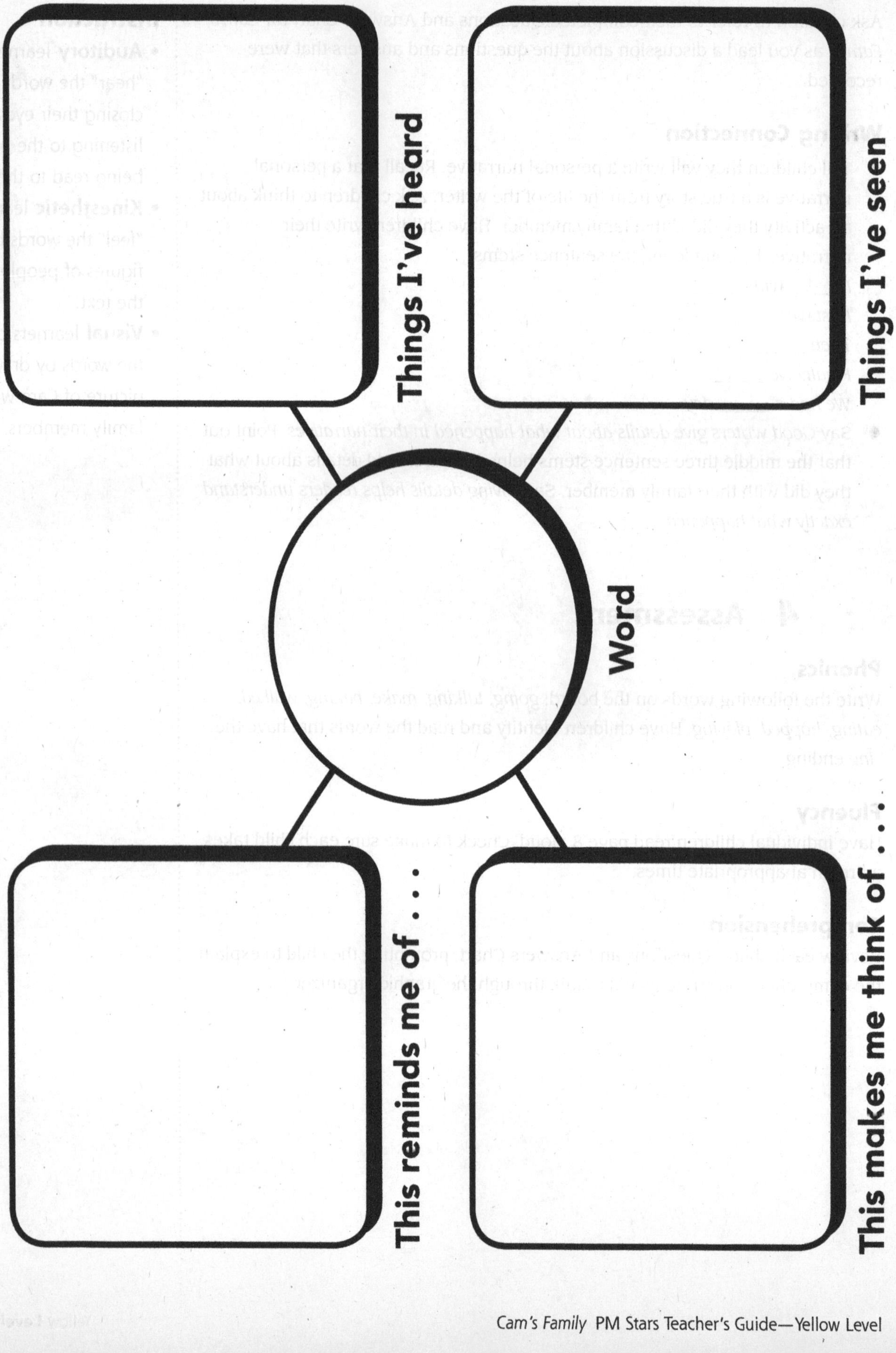

Things I've heard

Things I've seen

Word

This reminds me of …

This makes me think of …

Name _____

Questions and Answers Chart

Title _____

Questions	Answers

Anna's Family

Written by Debbie Croft   Photographs by Lindsay Edwards

Overview Anna lives with her mom, her dad, and her younger brother. Her mom grows flowers and her dad fixes cars. Her brother likes to play while Anna is in school. How does Anna help her family?

Reading Vocabulary Words town p. 4, garden p. 10, shop p. 10, tow p. 12, truck p. 12, mechanic p. 12, garage p. 12, safe p. 14

Vocabulary Skill Context clues

Phonological Awareness Skill Segmenting sounds

Fluency Point Reading every word; does not skip or substitute words

Comprehension Strategy Identifying main topic and key details

Reading Strategy Looking at the pictures

Writing Connection Report

Common Core State Standards RI.1.2 Identify the main topic and retell key details of a text; RF.1.2d Segment spoken single-syllable words into their complete sequence of individual sounds (phonemes); RF.1.4b Read grade-level text orally with accuracy, appropriate rate, and expression; W.1.2 Write informative/explanatory texts in which they name a topic, supply some facts about the topic, and provide some sense of closure; L.1.4a Use sentence-level context as a clue to the meaning of a word or phrase.

Reading Word Count: 164

High-Frequency Words

walk   play
they   help
of

More books in the family series

The Race
PM Stars Red Levels 5/6

Cam's Family
PM Stars Yellow Levels 8/9

Meg's Family
PM Stars Yellow Levels 8/9

Kris's Family
PM Stars Yellow Levels 8/9

Track
PM Stars Blue Levels 11/12

Running Races
PM Stars Green Levels 14/15

 **1 Before Reading**

Build Background

- Introduce the book by reading the title aloud with children. Point out the author's name. Say *What can you tell about this family from the photo? What do you think we'll find out about this family as we read?* Invite children to point out details and make predictions.

- Have children tell what they know about families. Ask *Who is in your family? What kind of job do the adults in your family have? How do you help them out?*

Focus on Reading Vocabulary

- Write the Reading Vocabulary words on the board. Read each word aloud and discuss with children its meaning. Guide children to think about how some of the words can be used together, such as *tow truck* and *garden shop*. Have children use pairs of words in sentences.

- Explain to children that the other words in a sentence may help them figure out the meaning of an unknown word or phrase. Say *These are called context clues.* Write the following sentence on the board: *When the grass gets too long, I have to mow it.* Ask children to tell how the other words in the sentence helped them figure out *mow*.

- Write the following sentence on the board: *I planted tomatoes and peppers in my garden.* Model filling out a Context Clues graphic organizer. Write *garden* in the top box. Have children identify words from the sentence that help them understand the meaning of *garden*. Write them in the middle box. Together, write the meaning of *garden* in the bottom box.

Focus on Phonological Awareness

Write *six* on the board. Say the word aloud slowly. Repeat the word, pointing to each sound represented by a letter. Guide children to segment the word into beginning, middle, and ending sounds. As the individual sounds are segmented have children tap their finger, for example /s/ /i/ /x/ would have three taps. Write and say the following one-syllable words, asking children to segment each sound: *pop, ray, van, most, high, black, send,* and *need.*

Focus on Fluency

Write on the board *I like to help my family work in the garden on the weekends.* Have children follow along as you read the sentence. Say *Good readers read every word that is written. They make sure not to skip words or say the wrong word.* Reread the sentence without one of the words, and again substituting *walk* for *work.* Point out that when words are skipped or changed, the sentence doesn't make sense.

Focus on Comprehension

Explain that nonfiction books are written to explore a topic. Say *The* topic *is the main idea that the book is about. The author includes information to help readers understand the topic. The most important details about the topic are called* key details. Display a familiar nonfiction book and guide children to identify the main topic and key details from the text.

2 Reading the Text

Have children read *Anna's Family.* As appropriate, monitor application of the comprehension strategy and support strategic reading using the prompts below.

Contents — Point to the title and explain that it is usually a clue to the main topic. Ask *What might the main topic of this book be?*

Pages 2–3 — Ask *Who are the people in Anna's family?* Point out that these are key details about the main topic of Anna's family.

Pages 4–5 — Point to the chapter heading. Ask *What do the details on this page tell about Anna's family?* Point out the vocabulary word *town.* Have children recall the meaning of the word. Ask *What do you think a small town is like?*

ESL/ELL

Sounding out words by segmenting them into their individual sounds is a necessary step in learning to decode. English language learners may have difficulty since they are still learning how to pronounce English words. Work with children to segment words such as *sit, but, big,* and *bus.* Ask them to watch your mouth as you say each word.

Reading Strategy

Explain to children that looking at the pictures is a helpful reading strategy. Have them look at the picture on page 3 and think about what they're seeing. Then have them read page 2, and then look at the picture again. Discuss how thinking about the picture helped them understand what they read.

High-Frequency Words

For children who need additional practice, use the appropriate cards from the *PM High-Frequency Word Cards* boxed set. Pair children and have them take turns reading and writing the high-frequency words.

Visual Literacy

Have children study the scene depicted on page 9. Ask *What word or phrase would you use to describe the overall mood or feeling of this photo?* Have children point to specific elements, such as use of color and body language, to support their responses.

Pages 6–7 Ask *Which person in Anna's family does this page give details about? What does Anna like to do?*

Pages 8–9 Have children recall the main topic of the book. Ask *What details on this page tell about the topic?* Ask children to read the page, making sure not to skip or substitute words.

Pages 10–11 Have children look at the chapter heading on page 8. Ask *Is this page still about Anna's mom? How do you know?* Point out the word *shop* and say it aloud. Ask *What is the beginning sound in shop? What is the middle sound? What is the ending sound?*

Pages 12–13 Ask *How are the details on this page about Anna's family?* Point to the vocabulary word *garage* in the third sentence. Have children find other words in the sentence that help them understand the meaning of *garage*.

Pages 14–15 Recall the prediction that Anna's family is the main topic of the book. Ask *Do you still think this is true? Why or why not? What does this page tell about Anna's family?*

Independent Practice

To further support application of the comprehension skill, have children reread the book using the Topic and Key Details graphic organizer for support. Assist children in filling in the organizer with the main topic and key details from the text. Observe children as they read. Make note of how each child is or is not using the skills and strategies being focused on in this lesson.

3 Review

Reading Vocabulary

- Provide children with the Context Clues organizer. Write *shop* in the top box. Work with children to find context clues in the second sentence on page 10. Model writing words that help them understand *shop* in the middle box. Then have children give a definition of *shop*. Write it in the bottom box.
- Have children highlight, or add, the reading vocabulary words in their copies of *My PM Word Book*. Encourage children to use these words in their writing.

Phonological Awareness

On chart paper, write *mat*. Say the word aloud and have children break it into its beginning, middle, and ending sounds. Then have them practice segmenting *fix, jog,* and *hus*.

Fluency

Remind children to make sure they don't skip over a word or substitute words as they read. Have pairs practice reading page 2 aloud, monitoring each other to make sure every word is read as written.

Comprehension

Ask children to refer to their completed Topic and Key Details chart for *Anna's Family* as you lead a discussion about the information that was recorded.

Writing Connection

- Tell children they will write a short report about their own families. Say *A report tells facts, or true information, about a topic.* Have children use the following sentence stems to write their report as appropriate:

    My family is _____.

    My mom _____.

    My dad _____.

    I have _____ sister(s).

    I have _____ brother(s).

    I help by _____.

- Say *In a report, it is important to tell your topic and give facts about the topic.* Point out that the first sentence tells about their family, which is what their report is about. Explain that their other sentences that tell how many brothers and/or sisters they have, how they contribute, and so on are facts about their family.

4 Assessment

Phonological Awareness

Have each child listen to two or three of the following words and segment them into their beginning, middle, and ending sounds: *cat, bed, big, not.*

Fluency

Have children read aloud pages 4 and 6 individually. Check to make sure they are not skipping over any words and are not substituting words.

Comprehension

Review each child's Topic and Key Details organizer, prompting the child to explain the comprehension strategy and to talk through the graphic organizer.

Differentiated Instruction

- **Kinesthetic** learners can "feel" the story by using puppets or dolls to act out the text.
- **Tactile** learners can "feel" the story by touching flowers from a garden and handling different kinds of mechanics' tools.
- **Visual** learners can "see" the story by thinking of something they learned about the characters and drawing a picture of one of them.

Name_____

Context Clues

- word I don't know

↓

- words that help me understand

↓

- word's meaning

Name_____

Topic and Key Details

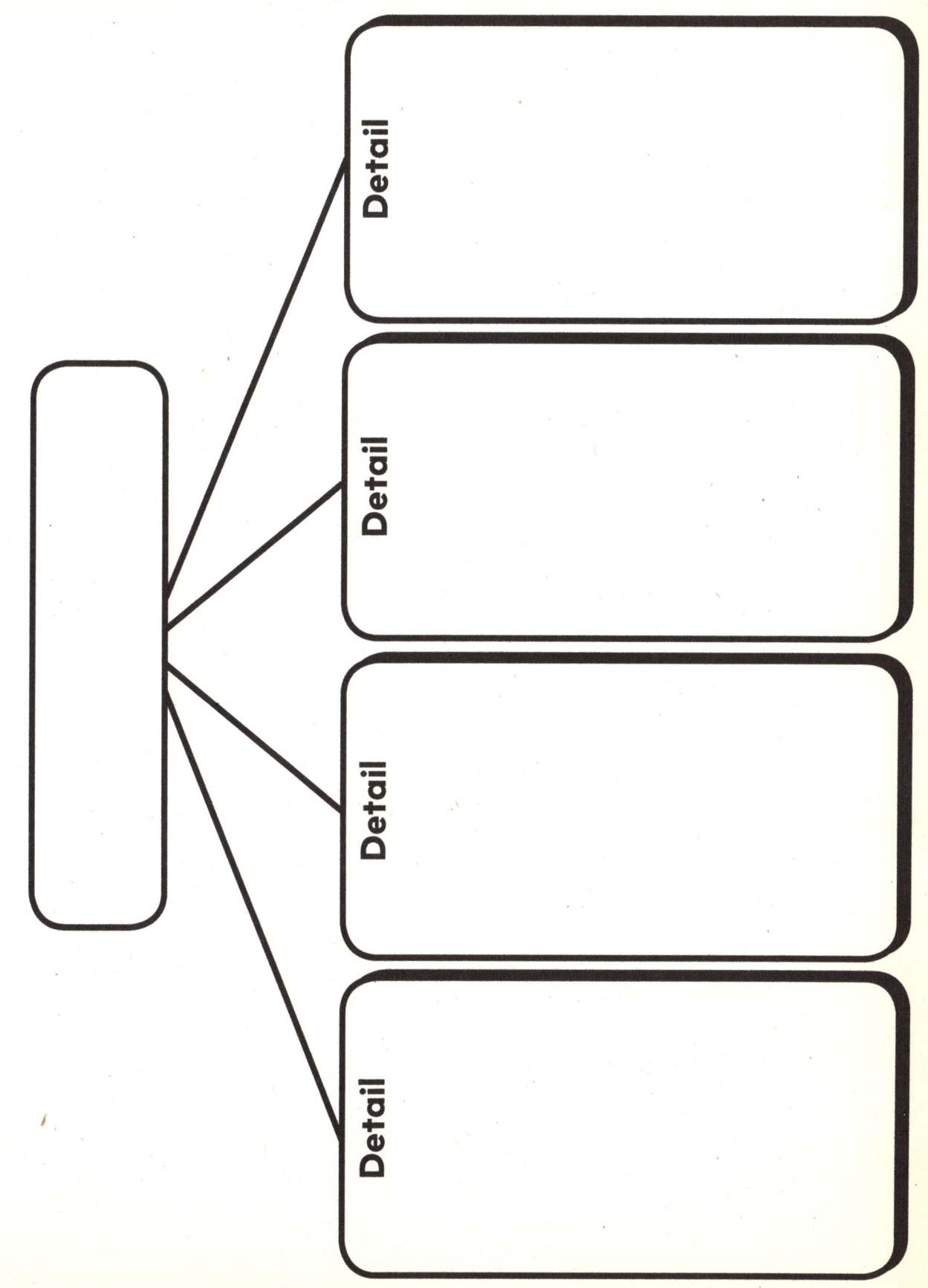

Anna's Family PM Stars Teacher's Guide—Yellow Level

109

Name _____

Topic and Key Details

- Detail
- Detail
- Detail
- Detail